Penguin Education

Penguin Education Special
General Editor: Willem van de

School is Dead
An Essay on Alternatives in Education
Everett Reimer

Everett Reimer has done too many things to mention in full: he
has sold maps, played professional football, printed greeting cards
and worked in a tyre factory. During the war he became a civil
servant. After that he worked for the Atomic Energy Commission,
for the Survey Research Center at the University of Michigan, and
for the Washington Research Center of the Maxwell School,
University of Syracuse.
Later he became Secretary of the Puerto Rican Committee of
Human Resources, and worked for the Alliance for Progress. He is
now, with Ivan Illich, at the Center for Intercultural Documentation
(CIDOC), and is Director of the CIDOC seminar on Alternatives
in Education.

School is Dead
An Essay on Alternatives in Education
Everett Reimer

Penguin Books

Penguin Books Ltd, Harmondsworth,
Middlesex, England
Penguin Books Australia Ltd,
Ringwood, Victoria, Australia

First published 1971
Copyright © Everett Reimer, 1971

Made and printed in Great Britain by
C. Nicholls & Company Ltd
Set in Monotype Plantin

Contents

My grandmother wanted me to have an education, so she kept me out of school.

MARGARET MEAD

Introduction

This book is the result of a conversation with Ivan Illich which has continued for fifteen years. We have talked of many things but increasingly about education and school and, eventually, about alternatives to schools.

Illich and I met in Puerto Rico, where I had come in 1954, as secretary of the committee on Human Resources of the Commonwealth Government, charged with assessing the manpower needs of the island and recommending an educational programme to meet them. Puerto Rico was then in the course of rapid industrialization and my calculations showed that dropout rates would have to decline throughout the school system if the estimated manpower needs of the economy were to be met. Everything was done to reduce these rates and they actually declined for a while, but it soon became apparent that the decline was at the expense of grade standards and, therefore, was meaningless.

Illich came to Puerto Rico in 1956, at the request of the late Cardinal Spellman, to organize a training programme for New York priests from parishes overrun by Puerto Rican migrants. We soon found common interests and many parallels in the problems of church and school. In 1960 Illich left Puerto Rico for Mexico,[1] and shortly after I also left for Washington to join the Alliance for Progress. We began to study the problems of Latin American education at about the same time and these turned out to be similar to the problems of Puerto Rico but on a vastly larger scale. It was soon clear to both of us that the countries of Latin America could not, for many years, afford schools for all of their children. At the same time education seemed to be the basic need of these countries, not only to us but to their political parties and leaders as well. In 1968 we began a part-time formal study of this dilemma and of possible ways out of it.

Our analysis of schools was soon extended to other institutions and to the structure of the society schools serve. At first we felt that school was a lagging institution in an increasingly efficient technological society. We later came to see schools as providing indispensable support for a technological society which is itself not viable. The simplest way to expose the contradictions of this society is to point out that it promises unlimited progress to unlimited numbers of people. The absurdity of this claim is conceded by the recognition of the need for birth control, but birth control itself turns out to depend on progress. Even at present rates of growth, by the time children can be kept in school long enough for schools to have a significant impact on birth rates, the population of the world will have increased threefold. And this is using conservative projections. If modern medical techniques were made generally available, the rate of population increase would double or triple.[2] We retain breathing space only by letting poor babies die at ten times the rate of privileged babies.

During the past decade the actual rate at which the benefits of modern institutions have been extended to the under-privileged peoples of the world is scarcely greater than the rate of population growth. On a *per capita* basis, individuals have benefited marginally, if at all.

Part of the problem lies in the inefficiency of modern institutions, including schools. The greater part lies in the promise of unlimited progress. As the world is now organized, the standard of living in India can rise only if the standard of living in the United States also rises. Yet a 3 per cent rise in the United States average income is twice the total income of the average Indian. Raising world consumption standards to US levels would multiply the combustion of fossil fuels by fifty times, the use of iron a hundred times, the use of other metals over two hundred times. By the time these levels were reached consumption levels in the United States would again have tripled and the population of the world would also have tripled. Such projections lead to results as absurd as the premises from which they start. There can be no open-ended progress. Yet this is what schools and other modern institutions promise. This is the promise of science and technology, unrestrained by reason. This is the promise which has bred schools and other modern institutions and which they in turn propagate. Schools are an essential element of a world in which technology is king.

The contradictions of such a world are becoming apparent. They are best illustrated in the school and best corrected by freeing education from the school so that people may learn the truth about the society in which they live.

In the course of the above analysis, an interpretation of human history has developed which, although sketchy and incomplete, must be shared with the reader. When techniques, institutions and ideologies were primitive, man lived in relative equality and freedom, because there were no adequate means of domination. As techniques, institutions and ideologies developed, they were used to establish and maintain relations of domination and privilege. From that time on, the societies which succeeded in dominating others, and thus world history, were also characterized by inter-class and inter-personal domination, in tension with efforts to establish equality. As techniques increased in efficiency and as ideologies gained in insight, they repeatedly threatened to upset the privilege structure of society. Institutions were used to counter these threats by controlling the use of the techniques and by perverting the ideologies. When revolutionary breakthroughs occurred, institutions were re-established on a broader base, extending privilege to more people, but always at the same time maintaining the structure of privilege. This view does not necessarily lead to a Jeffersonian suspicion of institutions as such. Despite the historical record, the possibility of democratic institutions remains – if men determine to use institutions for democratic purposes.

I would like to be able to say that the previous paragraph contains the last over-simplification in this book. Regrettably I cannot. I have tried to qualify my assertions, to provide evidence for them, to give supporting references and to justify my value judgements, but I do not expect to satisfy the norms of academic scholarship. To do that I would have to write not this book now but a completely different book twenty years from now. I chose to write this book now because I would like to live to see it become a self-fulfilling prophecy. Twenty years from now I might not be alive.

My view of history does not result in an unbiased appraisal of schools nor of the society to which schools belong, but rather in an indictment of both. Schools are admittedly treated in stereotype rather than in terms of concrete human behaviour. Schools are simply too big to treat concretely. Alternatives to school, as opposed to mere reform, require going beyond the experience of individuals to an analysis of the essential characteristics of schools. Nevertheless, in an abstract treatment people will not quite recognize themselves, as students, teachers, parents, or in other concrete roles related to schools. A few may feel themselves cast as the villains in a conspiracy of injustice. But this would be a misreading of the book.

There are unjust men in the world and it is an unjust world, but it is not the unjust men, primarily, who make it so. It is an unjust world largely because it is composed of faulty institutions. These institutions, in turn, are merely the collective habits of individuals, but individuals can have bad habits without being bad people. In general, people are unconscious of their habits, particularly their institutional habits. The positive thesis of this book is that people can become aware of their bad institutional habits and can change them. The world would then be a better world, made up of still imperfect people. There are, of course, some people who know that they have bad habits but do not want to change them. There are others who are afraid to examine their habits for fear that their consciences would then be troubled. This is the worst that can be said of most people. It is enough, however, to explain how the world can be worse than the people who live in it.

The realities of school are both better and worse than they are here described. Others have made more of an attempt at concrete portrayal and their work is an indispensable supplement to the present analysis. Tom Brown, Charlie Brown, Miss Peach and the children and teachers from George Dennison's[3] and Jonathan Kozol's[4] accounts are a few examples of attempts to show the reality of school. A model for general description and analysis of institutional behaviour is to be found in Floyd Allport's book by that name.[5] I regret that recognition of such a great teacher – encountered outside of school – should be accompanied by evidence of such poor learning.

This book owes far more debts than I can remember, let alone acknowledge. Several, however, must be singled out. Except for the insistence of Ralph Bohrson it might never have been written. Except for the help of the Ford Foundation travel and study grant which he administered, the time spent writing it might have been spent on other work. Cooperation from CIDOC, which has permitted me to work intensively with Illich, to publish earlier drafts and to discuss them with students and associates, has been even more vital. Many educators, economists, administrators and political leaders from Latin America, the United States and Europe have by this time participated in the analysis which Illich and I have conducted. Most of them are referred to in the text and in the appended notes. I want also to recognize the invaluable editorial assistance of Jordan Bishop, John Holt, Monica Raymond, Joan Remple, Dennis Sullivan and of many students at CIDOC with whom I have discussed earlier drafts. Not least is the debt I owe my wife and sons and daughters for years of critical conversation about education and the rest of life. None of my collaborators are directly responsible for anything in the book. Even Illich may disagree with parts of it. By the time it is published it is quite likely that I will too. (This sentence concluded the introduction to the first printed draft published by CIDOC, Cuernavaca, Mexico, in 1970. Four chapters of that draft have been jettisoned and eight new ones have been added. The sentence stands.)

Note for English Readers

In America the word 'school' is still used in what my English editors tell me is the medieval sense – i.e. to include any educational institution at any level, including universities. I use it in this sense.

We Americans are also backward in other ways. We still have to learn for example that the world is not our oyster. We still believe that revolutions are made primarily with guns. We still depend on a mixture of science and money to solve our serious problems. While these anachronisms are not unknown among the English-speaking peoples outside America they are, hopefully, somewhat less common and perhaps less virulent. I take this to reflect better experience rather than better genes. This experience – that there is a life after empire which one need not die to enjoy, this recent history of the British Empire – is the most substantial evidence available to support the notion of peaceful revolutionary change. Since peaceful revolution is my message, I have hopes that the barrier of terminology between me and my non-American English readers will be offset by the advantage of this superior history.

'If sharks were people,' his landlady's little daughter asked Mr K,
'would they be nicer to the little fish?' 'Of course,' he said,
'if sharks were people, they would have strong boxes built in the
sea for little fish. There they would put in all sorts of food, plants
and little animals, too. They would see to it that the boxes always
had fresh water, and they would take absolutely every sort of
sanitary measure. When, for example, a little fish would injure his
fin, it would be immediately bandaged so that he would not die on
the sharks before his time had come. In order that the little fish
would never be sad, there would be big water parties from time to
time; for happy fish taste better than sad ones. Of course, there
would be schools in the big boxes as well. There the little fish
would learn how to swim into the mouths of the sharks. They would
need, for example, geography so that they could find the sharks,
lazing around somewhere. The main subject would naturally be
the moral education of the little fish. They would be taught that the
grandest, most beautiful thing is for a little fish to offer himself
happily, and that they must all believe in the sharks, above all when
they say that they will provide for a beautiful future. One would
let the little fish know that this future is only assured when they
learn obedience. They must shy away from all lowly,
materialistic and Marxist inclinations, and inform the sharks
immediately if any one of them betrayed such tendencies. ...

If sharks were people, there would of course be art as well. There
would be beautiful pictures of sharks' teeth, all in magnificent
colours, of their mouths and throats as pure playgrounds where one
can tumble and play. The theatres on the bottom of the sea would
offer plays showing heroic little fish swimming enthusiastically
down the throats of the sharks, and the music would be so
beautiful that its sounds would lead the little fish dreamily to the
chapels and, filled with the most pleasant thoughts, they would
stream down the sharks' throats. There would certainly be religion.
... It would teach that true life really begins in the sharks' bellies.
And if sharks were people, the little fish would stop being, as they
are now, equals. Some would be given offices and be put over the
others. Those a little bigger would even be allowed to eat the
smaller ones. That would only be delightful for the sharks, for then
they would more often have bigger crumbs to gobble up. And the most
important of the little fish, those with offices, would look to the
ordering of the little fish. And they would become teachers, officers,
box-building engineers, etc. In short, there could only be culture
in the sea if the sharks were people.'

Bertolt Brecht: *Kalendergeschichten*

1 The Case Against Schools

Most of the children of the world are not in school. Most of those who enter drop out after a very few years. Most of those who succeed in school still become dropouts at a higher level. UNESCO data show that only in a small minority of nations do even half the children complete the first six grades.[1] No child, however, fails to learn from school. Those who never get in learn that the good things of life are not for them. Those who drop out early learn that they do not deserve the good things of life. The later dropouts learn that the system can be beat, but not by them. All of them learn that school is the path to secular salvation, and resolve that their children shall climb higher on the ladder than they did.[2]

For most members of the present generation this hope, that their children will benefit more from school than they, is doomed to disappointment. Schools are too expensive for this hope to be realized. For many, it may appear to be realized but the appearance will be a delusion, fostered by inflationary debasement of the academic currency. More college and high-school degrees will be granted but they will mean less, both in terms of amount and kind of learning and in terms of job qualification and real income.

In all countries, school costs are rising faster than enrolments and faster than national income. While the school's share of national income can afford to grow slowly as this income increases, it cannot continue to grow at present rates. In Puerto Rico, for example, the national income was ten times greater in 1965 than in 1940. School enrolment more than doubled during this period while school costs multiplied twenty-five times.[3] Yet, even in 1965, less than half of all Puerto Rican students finished nine years of school[4], and the proportion who reached the higher grades without learning to read was higher than it was twenty-five years earlier. Puerto Rico is atypical in its absolute rates of growth, but not in the vital relationships among them. Monographs on the cost of schooling in African and Asian countries, sponsored by the International Institute for Educational Planning, paint a similar picture, as do studies in Britain and most of the countries of western Europe.[5,6] Recent studies in the United States suggest that it would cost eighty billion additional dollars to meet educators' estimates of what is needed to provide adequate schooling.[7] Even the settlement of the war in Indochina would provide only a small fraction of this amount.

The conclusion is inescapable: no country in the world can afford the education its people want in the form of schools. Except for a few rich nations, and some not yet exposed to the development virus, no country in the world can afford the schools its people are now demanding from their political leaders. Continued attempts to supply the demand for college study in the United States will condemn the black and rural minorities to an indefinite wait for an adequate education. In India, Nigeria and Brazil the majority must, for generations, be denied all but marginal educational resources if a tiny minority is to enjoy the luxury of schooling, which would still be regarded as pitifully inadequate by United States standards. Development economists argue that peasants in India, sharecroppers in Alabama and dishwashers from Harlem do not need more education until the world is ready to absorb them into better jobs, and that these better jobs can be created only by others who must, therefore, be given educational priority.[8] But this argument ignores many of the economic, demographic and political facts of life. Economic growth, where it is occurring, principally bolsters the level of living of the already better off, fattens military and security-police budgets, and supports the markets of more developed nations. Population is growing so much faster than the rate at which real educational opportunities can be expanded by means of schools that deferring the education of the masses merely leaves a more difficult task for the future. On the other hand, people will not voluntarily curtail birth rates until they have a minimum not only of education but also of the social mobility which education implies.[9] If there were a monopoly of power in the world, population growth might be curtailed arbitrarily. In the world as it is, to ignore popular demands for education is not only morally indefensible, it is politically impossible, except by military governments. For most people, forcing others not to have children would be a completely unacceptable policy.

While children who never go to school are most deprived, economically and politically, they probably suffer the least psychological pain. Andean Indians, tribal Africans and Asian peasants belong to communities which have no schools or which have them only for the children of the élite. Their parents and grandparents have never known schools as places they expected their children to attend. They do know, however, what schools imply. Going to school means leaving the traditional life, moving to a different place, laying aside physical burdens for the work of the tongue and the mind, exchanging traditional food, clothing and customs for those of the larger town or distant city. Parents often prefer to keep the child in the traditional community, bearing the familiar burdens, confined to the enjoyments which primitive means can provide. They know, however, that this implies continuing domination by others, continuing dependence in times of hunger, war and sickness, increasing distance from those who enjoy wealth, power and respect. When the choice becomes a real one, most unschooled parents all over the world decide to send their children to school.

These first attenders have a harder time than their older brothers and sisters, for whom the school came too late. They do not last long in school. In 1960, half the children who entered school in Latin America never started the second grade, and half the second graders never started the third.[10] Three-fourths dropped out before they learned to read. They did learn, however, how unsuited they were to school, how poor their clothing was, how bad their manners, how stupid they were in comparison with those who went on to higher grades. This helped them accept the greater privilege and power of the deserving minority and their own relative poverty and political impotence. Yet they were not as ready as their older brothers and sisters to accept the limitations of their traditional lot. A little schooling can induce a lot of dissatisfaction. The more schooling a dropout has, the more it hurts him to drop out. The child who never learns to read can still accept his inferiority as a fact of life. The child who goes on to higher grades may learn that he is really no different from the sons of the mayor, the merchant or the school teacher, except that they have the money or the influence needed to go on to secondary school or college, while he must stay behind for lack of it. For him, it is much harder to accept their getting the better jobs, enjoying the higher offices, winning the more beautiful girls, all because they were able to stay in school longer than he.

A winner's world? If this were all, schools might still be defended; but the winners of the school game are a strange lot. The Ottomans used to geld their candidates for managerial posts. Schools make physical emasculation unnecessary by doing the job more effectively at the libidinal level. This is, of course, a simplistic metaphor. While there is evidence that girls do better in school than boys and that boys do less well the more masculine they are, this undoubtedly results more from social than from physical factors. The metaphor understates rather than overstates the facts. School domesticates – socially emasculates – both girls and boys by a process much more pervasive than mere selection by sex. School requires conformity for survival and thus shapes its students to conform to the norms for survival.[11] If learning the official curriculum of the school were the principal criterion, this might still not be so bad, although it would substitute the learning of what Whitehead and other philosophers of education have called dead knowledge for true learning. The actual survival criteria are much worse. In addition to the wealth or influence of parents, they include the ability to beat the game, which, according to John Holt and other perceptive teachers, is mainly what successful students learn in school.[12] Or, as H. L. Mencken put it, the main thing children learn in school is how to lie. This can hardly be avoided when survival in school ever more determines the degree of privilege and power which the student will enjoy as an adult.

To say that schools teach conformity and also teach students to beat the game is not contradictory. Beating the game is one form of conformity. Individual teachers may be concerned with what children learn, but school systems record only the marks they get. Most students learn to follow the rules which schools can enforce and to break those they cannot. But also, different students learn in varying degrees to conform, to ignore the rules and to take advantage of them. Those who ignore them in the extreme become dropouts, and learn mainly that they do not belong in school or in the society it represents. Those who conform to the rules become the dependable producers and consumers of the technological society. Those who learn to beat the school game become the exploiters of this society. Those on whom the discipline of the school falls lightly, who easily perform its assignments and have little need to violate its rules, are least touched by school. They are, or become, the social aristocrats and the rebels. This, at any rate, is what happened before schools began to break down. Now all kinds of students join in the rush for the door, while schools engage in a similar scramble to recapture their dropouts by any means.

As late as the turn of the century schools were still a minor institution and all who were not suited for them had other educational options. Fifty years ago, no country in the world had 10 per cent of its teenage population in school. Schools have grown so fast partly because they happened to be doing what was important to a technological era when this era began. Their monopoly of education has been achieved as one aspect of the monopoly of technology. The main reason we need alternatives to schools is because they close the door to humanity's escape from this monopoly. They ensure that those who inherit influence in a world dominated by technology will be those who profit by this domination and, even worse, those who have been rendered incapable of questioning it. Not only the leaders but their followers are shaped by the school game to play the game of competitive consumption – first to meet and then to surpass the standards of others. Whether the rules are fair or the game worth playing is beside the point.

School has become the universal church of a technological society, incorporating and transmitting its ideology, shaping men's minds to accept this ideology, and conferring social status in proportion to its acceptance. There is no question of man's rejecting technology. The question is only one of adaptation, direction and control. There may not be much time, and the only hope would seem to lie in education – the true education of free men capable of mastering technology rather than being enslaved by it, or by others in its name.

There are many roads to enslavement, only a few to mastery and freedom. Technology can kill by poisoning the environment, by modern warfare, by over-population. It can enslave by chaining men to endless cycles of competitive consumption, by means of police states, by creating dependence on modes of production which are not viable in the long run. There are no certain roads of escape from these dangers. There can be no road of escape at all, however, if men remain enthralled in a monolithic secular orthodoxy. The first amendment to the Constitution of the United States was a landmark in history. 'There shall be no establishment of religion.' Only the terms and the scope of the problem have changed. Our major threat today is a world-wide monopoly in the domination of men's minds.

I learned something in school today.
I signed up for folk guitar, computer programming, stained glass art, shoemaking and a natural foods workshop.
I got Spelling, History, Arithmetic and two study periods.

So what did you learn?

I learned that what you sign up for and what you get are two different things.

Charles Schulz: *Peanuts*

2 What Schools Do

Schools are supposed to educate. This is their ideology, their public purpose. They have gone unchallenged, until recently, partly because education is itself a term which means such different things to different people. Different schools do different things, of course, but increasingly, schools in all nations, of all kinds, at all levels, combine four distinct social functions: custodial care, social-role selection, indoctrination, and education as usually defined in terms of the development of skills and knowledge. It is the combination of these functions which makes schooling so expensive. It is conflict among these functions which makes schools educationally inefficient. It is also the combination of these functions which tends to make school a total institution, which has made it an international institution, and which makes it such an effective instrument of social control.

Custodial care is now so universally provided by schools that it is hard to remember earlier arrangements. Children must, of course, be cared for – if they really are children, that is, and not just young members of the community taking part in its normal productive and social affairs. Most youngsters still get along without special care, all over the world, in the tribal, peasant and urban dwellings of the poor.[1]

Child care costs money, and although schools provide it relatively cheaply, this is where most of the school budget goes.[2] Time studies conducted in Puerto Rico by Anthony Lauria show that less than 20 per cent of a teacher's time is available for instructional activities. The rest is spent on behaviour control and administrative routine. Lauria's data support a statement John Gardner once made, long before he was Secretary of Health, Education and Welfare in the federal government of the United States. He said that everything a high-school graduate is taught in twelve years of schooling could easily be learned in two

years and with a little effort in one. Since child care is the most
tangible service schools provide, and since parents are naturally
concerned about the quality of such care, this function has a
priority claim on school resources. Other functions must compete
for what is left after prevailing local standards of safety, comfort
and convenience have been met.

As children get older, child care, paradoxically, becomes both
more extensive and more expensive. Actual hours spent in
school increase, buildings are more luxurious, the ratio of paid
adults to students increases, and the salaries of these adults also
increase. Where there are no schools, children contribute more
to the community and require less support as they grow older.[3]
High schools, however, take more of the students' time than
primary schools, and cost more too, while most colleges and
universities occupy the full time of the student, at an ever
increasing hourly cost, as students progress up the academic
ladder. The costs of higher education, admittedly, cover more
than mere custodial care, but at upper as well as lower levels,
the time students spend in school is an important cost factor.
Space is also costly; the commodious college campus, insulated
from the non-academic environment, is much more expensive
than the neighbourhood kindergarten.

Money, however, is the least of the costs of providing custodial
care in schools. The really important consequence of packaging
custody with the other functions of the school is the extension
of childhood from age twelve to twenty-five, and from the sons
and daughters of the rich to the youth of the whole society. This,
in turn, is only one aspect of the division of modern life into
school, work and retirement.

So long as children remain full-time students they remain
children – economically, politically, even legally. While no formal
legal sanctions are available against students, as such, they can
always be deprived of their rights to schooling, and thus to
preferred employment and social status. The school schedule
remains, also, one of the major supports for age restrictions on
the right to vote, to work, to contract and to enjoy other con-
stitutional privileges and protections. The school itself, as
custodian of ever larger numbers of people, for increasing pro-
portions of their life span, for an ever growing number of hours

and interests, is well on the way to joining armies, prisons and insane asylums as one of society's total institutions. Strictly speaking, total institutions are those which totally control the lives of their inmates, and even armies, prisons and asylums do this completely only for certain inmates. Only vacation-less boarding schools could strictly be called total institutions, but perhaps the strict definition gives too much attention to the body and too little to the mind and spirit. Schools pervade the lives and personalities of their students in powerful and insidious ways and have become the dominant institution in the lives of modern men during their most formative years.

Studies of prisons and asylums indicate how overwhelmingly such institutions produce the very behaviour they are designed to correct. In one experiment, almost all the members of a group of persons diagnosed as hopelessly insane, asylum inmates for over twenty years, were discharged as cured within a few months of being placed in a 'normal' environment. In another experiment, a group of persons diagnosed as dangerously insane were allowed to institute self-government among themselves and managed without incident.[4] A similar cure for student unrest would be to stop making children out of people old enough to have children, support them and fight for them. This would, of course, require other social changes in addition to the divorce of custodial care from education at the higher levels of schooling, but they are equally necessary changes if society is to survive.

A second function of schools, more directly in conflict with their educational aims than custodial care, is the sorting of the young into the social slots they will occupy in adult life. Some of this sorting occurs at the high-school and college level, when students begin to opt for this or that profession or trade and enter special curricula of one to a dozen years in length for vocational preparation. The results of even this accepted aspect of job selection in school are wasteful and often disastrous. Part of the waste is in the high proportion of dropouts, not only from professional and trade schools but from the professions and trades themselves, frequently after long and expensive investments have been made. Many people find that medicine or teaching is not for them – something they could have found out much sooner and much cheaper if they had begun as orderlies, nurses or teachers' aides. Even those who stay in the field of their choice do not escape extensive waste of time and money. According to the folklore of many occupations, the first several years of work are spent forgetting what was learned about the vocation in school. Counselling and many other sincere and systematic efforts are made to minimize this kind of waste but it is doubtful that, even at great additional cost, they can do more than slow its acceleration. The ever greater separation of school from the rest of life widens a gap which no amount of effort can bridge.

The major part of job selection is not a matter of personal choice at all, but a matter of survival in the school system. Age at dropout determines whether boys and girls will be paid for their bodies, hands or brains and also, of course, how much they will be paid. This in turn will largely determine where they can live, with whom they can associate, and the rest of their style of life. Within this century, any profession could still be entered at the bottom. Today this is difficult even in countries which provide schools for only a tiny minority. In the United States, it is now hard to become a carpenter without having graduated from high school. In New York City even a garbage collector needs a diploma.

While economic status is largely a function of the level at which a student drops out, power in the society depends more upon the sorting that occurs when high-school graduates enter college. Admission to Harvard College practically guarantees access to the groups which will control the major hierarchies of the United States. State and local as well as national hierarchies are the products of the college lottery. Even international agencies are ruled by the graduates of a dozen world-famous universities.

Power and wealth are not everything, of course, but almost everything else depends upon them in many parts of the world. Especially where the school system is dominant, respect, reputation, health, even affection of many kinds, can either be commanded or purchased – if they are not tendered as gifts to those who could order or buy them.

The school system has thus amazingly become, in less than a century, the major mechanism for distributing values of all kinds among all the peoples of the world, largely replacing the family, the church and the institution of private property in this capacity. In capitalist countries it might be more accurate to say that schools confirm rather than replace the value-distribution functions of these older institutions. Family, religion and property have such an important influence on access to and success in school that schooling alters only slowly and marginally the value distributions of an earlier day. Jefferson put it well when he said, in arguing for public schools, that by this means we shall each year rake a score of geniuses from the ashes of the masses. The result of such a process, as the English aristocracy learned long before Jefferson, is to keep the élite alive while depriving the masses of their potential leaders.

Communist countries have, of course, abolished private property, have attempted to abolish organized religion and have tried to weaken the role of the family. There are few data, unfortunately, to show how much redistribution of values has taken place in these countries but the general impression is that it is much less than had been expected. One of the strongest supports for this impression comes from the great similarity of school systems in capitalist and communist countries. They perform the same functions and share the same defining characteristics. There is not the slightest doubt that communist schools sort their students into jobs, vocational levels, pay differentials, power and privilege strata in just the same way as capitalist schools. The only question is whether the prizes go to the sons and daughters of the previously privileged in quite the same degree.

Leaders in communist China are greatly preoccupied with this question. In 1966, schools throughout China were closed for over a year in an attempt to make education more egalitarian and down to earth. Mao's own policy statements make clear his desire to rid education of élite control and to make it universally available to the masses. The difficulties encountered in this effort are obviously formidable, however, even for Mao, and it appears that most schools reopened in 1967 with significant but not really fundamental changes in the structure of the system. How much of this compromise was due to ideological and how much to practical considerations is hard to say. The pressures of building a nation in competition with such super-powers as

Russia and the United States must be tremendous, and schools appear to be an almost indispensable tool for nation building. On the other hand, the educational controversy in China has never abandoned the rhetoric of schools. Despite all the emphasis on universal access, practicality and revolutionary objectives, the debate always refers to the reform of the school system rather than to its replacement.[5]

It should now be clear why schools have grown so fast. To the masses, and their leaders, they have held out unprecedented hope of social justice. To the élite they have been an unparalleled instrument, appearing to give what they do not, while convincing all that they get what they deserve. Only the great religions provide an analogy, with their promise of universal brotherhood always betrayed.

Betrayal of the hopes of schooling is implicit in the selection function which schools perform. Selection implies losers as well as winners and, increasingly, selection is for life. Furthermore, school is a handicap race in which the slower must cover a greater distance bearing the growing burden of repeated failure, while the quicker are continually spurred by success. Nevertheless, the finish line is the same for all and the first to get there win the prizes. All attempts to disguise the reality of this situation fail. Parents know the truth, while teachers and administrators are often compelled to admit it. Euphemisms about the transcendent importance of learning and about doing your best are, thus, self-defeating. It is no wonder, under these circumstances, that some children drop out while others work to win rather than to learn.

Consistently punishing half of the children who are trying to learn what society is trying to teach them is not the worst aspect of combining social-role selection with education. Such punishment is an unavoidable result of the relative failure which half the school population must experience while climbing the school ladder in competition with their more successful peers. Such punishment can scarcely help but condition this half of the school population to resist all future efforts to induce them to learn whatever is taught in school. But this is only the lesser evil. The greater is that school necessarily sorts its students into a caste-like hierarchy of privilege. There may be nothing wrong with hierarchy nor with privilege, nor even with hierarchies of privilege, so long as these are plural and relatively independent of each other. There is everything wrong with a dominant hierarchy of privilege to which all others must conform. Birth into a caste, inheritance of wealth and the propagation of a governing party are all means by which such a dominant hierarchy can be maintained. In the modern technological world, however, all of these means either depend upon or are replaced by the school. No single system of education can have any other result nor can a dominant hierarchy of privilege be maintained in a technological world by any means except a unified system of education.

If schools continue for a few more generations to be the major means of social-role selection, the result will be a meritocracy, in which merit is defined by the selection process that occurs in schools. Michael Young describes this outcome in his *Rise of the Meritocracy*.[6] His picture of English society, fifty years from now, is a projection of Galbraith's New Industrial State with the technocrats in the saddle.[7] He describes a school system which becomes a super-streaming system, constantly shuffling its students into the channels where their past performance suggests that they belong. The slow students are not kidded in this system; they quickly learn where they stand and where they are going, but they are taught to like it. The quick also know where they are going and like it so well they end up trying to re-establish an hereditary aristocracy based on merit. This reverse English twist leads to a happy ending which takes humanity off the hook, but not until the author has made his – and repeated Dante's – point. Any system in which men get just what they deserve is Hell.

Schools define merit in accordance with the structure of the society served by schools. This structure is characterized by the competitive consumption of technological products defined by institutions. Institutions define products in a way which is consistent with the maintenance of a dominant hierarchy of privilege and, as far as possible, with the opportunity for members of the currently privileged class to retain their status in the new 'meritocracy'.

What schools define as merit is principally the advantage of having literate parents, books in the home, the opportunity to travel, etc. Merit is a smoke screen for the perpetuation of privilege. The ability of I Q tests to predict school performance does not rebut this statement. As Arthur Jensen, the most recent defender of I Q, points out, the intelligence measured by tests is operationally defined as the ability to succeed in school.[8] The significance of Michael Young's book is to show that merit is an ideological as well as an actual smoke screen; that we would be even worse off if 'true merit' were to replace more primitive means of perpetuating privilege.

The third function of schooling is indoctrination. Indoctrination is a bad word. Bad schools, we say, indoctrinate. Good ones teach basic values. All schools, however, teach the value of childhood, the value of competing for the life prizes offered in school and the value of being taught – not learning for one's self – what is good and what is true.[9] In fact, all schools indoctrinate in ways more effective than those which are generally recognized.

By the time they go to school, children have learned how to use their bodies, how to use language and how to control their emotions. They have learned to depend upon themselves and have been rewarded for initiative in learning. In school these values are reversed. The what, when, where and how of learning are decided by others, and children learn that it is good to depend upon others for their learning. They learn that what is worthwhile is what is taught and, conversely, that if something is important someone must teach it to them.

Children learn in school not only the values of the school but to accept these values and, thus, to get along in the system. They learn the value of conformity and, while this learning is not confined to school, it is concentrated there. School is the first highly institutionalized environment most children encounter. For orphans and children who are sick or handicapped this is not the case, and the retarding effects of institutionalizing infants is impressively documented.[10] Orphans learn so well not to interfere with institutional requirements that they seldom become capable of making a useful contribution to society. The argument for schools, of course, is that they strike the balance between conformity and initiative which the institutional roles of adult life will require.

Other values are implicit in those aspects of curriculum which are alike in schools all over the world. These include the priorities given to dominant languages, both natural and technical. Examples of the first are the priority given to Spanish over Indian tongues in Latin America, and to Russian over provincial languages in the Soviet Union. Examples of the second are the priorities given mathematics over music, and physics over poetry. There are obviously good reasons for these priorities, but they are reasons derived from the world as it is, ignoring the claims of both the world of the past and the desirable world of the future. More than this, these decisions reflect not even all of the major aspects of today's world, but preponderantly the balance of political and economic power. Less people speak English than Chinese and far fewer speak physics than poetry. English and physics are simply more powerful – at the moment.

Another value implicit in school is that of hierarchy. Schools both reflect dominant values and maintain a stratified world. They make it seem natural and inevitable that hierarchies are inherently correlated and cannot be independent of each other. Schools do not have to teach this doctrine. It is learned by studying an integrated curriculum arranged in graded layers.

Finally, after performing child care, social screening and value-teaching functions, schools also teach cognitive skills and both transmit and – at graduate levels – create knowledge. The first three functions are performed necessarily, because of the way schools are organized. Cognitive learning, although it is declared the principal purpose of schools, occurs only in so far as resources remain after the in-built functions are performed. In urban ghetto schools of the United States and in rural Brazilian schools, attempting to operate on a budget of fifty dollars per year per child, very little cognitive learning occurs.[11,12] Of course exceptional teachers can teach and exceptional students can learn within the confines of the school. As school systems expand, claiming an increasing proportion of all educational resources, absorbing more students and teachers and more of the time of each, some true educational experiences are bound to occur in schools. They occur, however, despite and not because of school.[13]

Schools rest much of their case on their claim to teach skills, especially language and mathematical skills. The most commonly heard defence of schools is 'Where else would children learn to read?' Literacy has, in fact, always run well ahead of schooling. According to census data, there are always more literate members of a society than persons who have gone to school. Furthermore, where schooling is universal, there are always children attending school who do not learn to read. In general, the children of literate parents learn to read even if they do not attend school, while the children of illiterate parents frequently fail to learn even in school.[14]

In universally schooled societies, of course, most children learn to read in school. Considering when they learn to read and when they begin to go to school, it could hardly be otherwise. Even in a fully schooled society, however, few children learn to read easily and well, although almost all learn to speak easily and well, a skill learned outside of school.[15] Children who do learn to read well read a lot for their own pleasure, which suggests that good reading – like other skills – is the result of practice. Data on mathematics give even less support to school. Illiterates who participate in a money economy all learn to count, add, subtract, multiply and divide, while only a small percentage of people in a fully schooled society ever learn much more. Of those who take algebra in high school, only a small percentage do better than chance on an objective test.[16]

There is a body of data collected by Jerome Bruner and his students showing that children who go to school learn concepts which are not learned by those who do not go to school.[17] The concepts studied were those made famous by Jean Piaget, who found that most French and Swiss children learn at about ages six to eight that water poured from a short fat cylinder into a tall thin one is still the same amount of water. Bruner's students found that African bush children who go to schools which are patterned after the French, learn such concepts much better than similar children who do not go to school. These experiments did not, however, test the effect of relevant learning environments other than school. Until a unique effect of schooling is demonstrated, with everything else controlled, Bruner's data show only that environments affect concept learning and suggest that the more relevant the environment is to the concept the more effect it has.

Another claim is that schools teach the grammar of language, the theories of mathematics, science and the arts. Undoubtedly they do; but the real question is whether these things are learned in school more than they would be otherwise. Achievement tests give little support to schools. As in the case of mathematics, only a small minority of students do better than chance on the formal aspects of any subject matter. Students who are interested in these matters learn them and those who are not do not. Whether interest in them is stimulated by schools remains very doubtful. Einstein, commenting upon a short period he had to spend in school preparing for a degree examination, said that as a consequence he was, for several years afterwards, unable to do any creative work.

The pernicious effect of schools on cognitive learning, of which Einstein complains, is best seen by contrasting the impact of schooling on privileged and underprivileged children. The underprivileged, whose home environments are lacking in the specialized resources schools provide, are relatively unsuccessful in school and soon leave it with an experience of failure, a conviction of inadequacy and a dislike for the specialized learning resources of which they are subsequently deprived. The privileged, whose home environments are rich in the specialized resources of the school, who would learn on their own most of what the school has to teach, enjoy relative success in school and become hooked on a system which rewards them for learning without the exercise of effort or initiative. Thus, the poor are deprived both of motivation and of the resources which the school reserves for the privileged. The privileged, on the other hand, are taught to prefer the school's resources to their own and to give up self-motivated learning for the pleasures of being taught. The minorities of Einsteins and Eldridge Cleavers lose only a little time. The majority lose their main chance for an education.

First-hand knowledge is the ultimate basis of intellectual life. To a large extent book-learning conveys second-hand information, and as such can never rise to the importance of immediate practice.... What the learned world tends to offer is one second-hand scrap of information illustrating ideas derived from another second-hand scrap of information. The second-handedness of the learned world is the secret of its mediocrity. It is tame because it has never been scared by facts.

Alfred North Whitehead: *The Aims of Education and Other Essays*

3 What Schools Are

It may seem academic to distinguish what schools do from what schools are, but the purpose of the distinction is very practical. Alternatives to schools cannot be formulated unless we can define school. Schools perform necessary social functions which, in some form and combination, always have to be performed. Some people believe that schools can be reformed while others hold that no specialized alternatives to schools are needed, since all the education men require can come as a by-product of their other activities. Neither position can be refuted or properly evaluated without a definition of school. The reasons for defining schools are heuristic; to know better what to do and what to avoid in planning alternatives. Precision, therefore, is less important in the definition than usefulness in practice. We define schools as *institutions which require full-time attendance of specific age groups in teacher-supervised classrooms for the study of graded curricula.* The better this definition fits an institution the more nearly does the institution correspond to the stereotype of school. Alternatives in education can be most generally defined as moving away from this stereotype. Unless they move far enough and fast enough, however, to escape the 'gravitational pull' of the school system, they will be re-absorbed.

By specifying the age of required attendance, schools institutionalize childhood. In schooled societies, childhood is now assumed to be a timeless and universal phenomenon. But children, in the modern sense, did not exist three hundred years ago and still do not exist among the rural and urban poor who make up most of the population of the world. In his *Centuries of Childhood* Phillipe Ariès shows that, before the seventeenth century, children dressed as adults, worked with adults, were imprisoned, tortured and hanged like adults, were exposed to sex, disease and death, and in general did not have a special status. The sub-culture of childhood did not exist.[1] The medieval church assumed that children, baptized in infancy, reached the age of reason at about the age of seven; this meant that they were from then on fully responsible for their acts, not only to men but to God. They were capable, that is, either by positive acts or by neglect, of consigning themselves to everlasting torment. In its time this doctrine was not unique. Children were treated no more tenderly in the Arab or Oriental worlds or, for that matter, in Africa or America.

All cultures, of course, distinguish infants and sexually immature youth from adults. All cultures have initiation rites which signal entrance into full adult status. All cultures make some distinction between what adults and non-adults may do and have done to them. This is not to say, however, that all cultures have a sub-culture of childhood. Children in the western culture are not expected to work, except at their studies. Children are not responsible for any nuisance, damage or crime they commit upon society. Children do not count, legally or politically. Children are supposed to play, enjoy themselves and prepare themselves for adult life. They are supposed to go to school, and the school is supposed to be responsible for them, guide them and, temporarily at least, take the place of their parents. Childhood explains the priority which schools give to custodial care.

Childhood must also be viewed in contrast with modern, pre-retirement adult life. Childhood and the adult world of work have been drawing apart. While children have been increasingly indulged, pre-retirement adults – women as well as men – have been increasingly moulded to the world of machines and institutions. Childhood has become more child-centred, more indulgent, while adults have been increasingly constrained. The argument for schools is that they provide a necessary bridge from childhood to adult life, that they gradually transform the indulged child into the responsible adult. Schools take the child from his garden, by carefully graded steps, to a prototype of the world of work. They enrol the 'complete child' and graduate the 'complete man'.

As in the case of the school, childhood has probably served a useful purpose. The pre-childhood treatment of children was, and is, undesirably brutal. Many of the protections childhood has brought to children are important and necessary – so much so that it is vital to extend them, not only to other children, but also to adults. Sexual abuse, under conditions which make consent a farce, is one example. The exploitation of labour under similar conditions is another: one party has the choice of working or starving while the other has to choose merely between one labourer and another. The enforcement or neglect of conditions which stunt the growth or unnecessarily limit the opportunities of children, or adults, need to be prohibited and prevented wherever they occur. But this is impossible if the indulgence of already indulged children is endlessly multiplied. Furthermore, while some protections and indulgences are necessary and good, too many are bad, and we have reached and passed many thresholds in the institution of childhood at which benefits become liabilities. Many of these are obvious and need no argument. One which has already been noted is the extension of the age of childhood to include fully mature adults, so long as these adults remain in school. Much of the protest on the part of youth is related to this fact, as is the resentment by adults of this protest. The case for youth is obvious. Old enough to have children of their own and to fight for them, they are encouraged to do only the latter and are denied the right to participate fully in the economic product of the society. The adult case is also easy to understand. These children, they say, want to remain children and yet to enjoy the privileges of adults. In part, the adults are right. What they forget is that youth did not create the institution of childhood but were created by it.

Schools, as creators of social reality, do not stop with children. They also create school teachers. Before there were schools there were caretakers of children, gymnastic disciplinarians enforcing practice, and masters with disciples.[2] None of these three assumed that learning resulted from teaching, while schools treat learning as if it were the *product* of teaching.

The role of the school teacher in this process is a triple one, combining the functions of umpire, judge and counsellor. As umpire, the teacher rules answers right or wrong, assigns grades and decides upon promotion. As judge, the teacher induces guilt in those who cheat, neglect their homework, or otherwise fail to live up to the moral norms of the school. As counsellor, the teacher hears excuses for failure to meet either academic or moral standards and counsels the student on choices to be made both inside the school and out. This description fails to sound strange only because students are regarded as people without civil rights. Imagine combining the role of policeman, judge and attorney for the defence – or the role of buyer, appraiser and economic counsellor – or the role of referee, athletic commissioner and coach. In a purely formal sense, the student in this situation is helpless, while the teacher is omnipotent.

In American schools the teacher is obviously not omnipotent. Almost the reverse seems to be true. How can this be explained? Teachers have the roles and powers described above. They also exercise them, but usually not effectively. This is because the system has broken down, but the breakdown is itself inherent in the distortion which school creates in the true roles of the teacher. As suggested above, these were exemplified in the pre-school era: in the Greek slave who safeguarded his young charges in their excursions about the city, in the disciplinarian who kept them at their practice of arms, in the master prepared to dispute with them in matters of politics, ethics and philosophy. Of these, only the disciplinarian survived without major distortion in the early schools. Drill with the pen rather than the sword involved only a change of instrument, and the method was equally effective. Schools stopped being effective in teaching skills when this method was abandoned. The other two roles were totally distorted in their incorporation into school. The caretaker role depended completely for its educational validity upon not overstepping its bounds. The caretaker slave had nothing to say about place, time or activity except to keep his charges within the bounds of safety. The educational value of the activities depended upon student selection and conduct. The master was also transformed into his opposite when placed within the school. His true role was to be questioned and to answer in such a way as to provoke ever deeper questions. In the school, this role is reversed – the master becomes the questioner and is forced to propound orthodoxy rather than provoke exploration.

Children and teachers do not yet make a school. Without required attendance in specialized space, teachers and children could be a home, a nursery or a crusade. Required classroom attendance adds the time and space dimensions which imply that knowledge can be processed and that children have an assigned time and place. During infancy they belong in the home. At kindergarten age they begin to belong, for a few hours a day, in school. The amount of school time increases with age, until college becomes Alma Mater, sacred or soul mother, the social womb in which the child develops and from which he is finally delivered into the adult world. Classrooms may be varied to include laboratory, workshop, gymnasium and year abroad, but this is all scholastic space – sanitized, sealed off from the unclean world, made fit for children and for the transmission of knowledge. In this specialized environment, knowledge must be transmitted, it cannot merely be encountered, since in most instances it has been taken out of its natural habitat. It must also be processed, not only to clean it up but also to facilitate transmission.

The transmission of knowledge through teaching, and its processing to fit school and school children, seems perfectly natural in a technological age which engineers a product to fit every human need. Once knowledge becomes a product, the graded curriculum follows – an ordered array of packets of knowledge each with its time and space assignment, in proper sequence and juxtaposed with related packages. The graded curriculum is the fourth dimension of the school. As in the case of the other defining characteristics, its quantitative aspects are critically important. Childhood becomes a problem when extended over too many years and too many aspects of life. Teaching becomes a problem when students begin to depend upon it for most learning. Classroom attendance becomes a problem when it builds sterile walls around too much of normal life. Similarly, curriculum becomes a problem as it approaches international universality. How much required attendance, classroom teaching and curriculum is tolerable is not a matter for academic discussion. Free people, choosing freely as individuals and in voluntary groups among an ample array of alternatives, can best make these decisions.

Recent international achievement studies demonstrate quite clearly that the universal international curriculum is now a fact.[3] International norms for mathematics and science have been established. These are admittedly the areas of greatest

uniformity but others are not far behind. Nor is the proliferation of vocational schools, black studies and life-adjustment
classes a significant counter-trend. These auxiliary curricula are
either tied to the core curriculum, in terms of prerequisites and
grade standards, or else the degrees they lead to are meaningless
in the market place.

The graded curriculum may be the most significant charac-
teristic of the school, especially in terms of the school's role in
society. This, however, is only because the curriculum is the
keystone of a system based on institutionalized childhood, teaching and classroom attendance. Curriculum gives structure to
these other elements, uniting them in a way which determines
the unique impact of school on students, teachers and society.

In itself, the central idea of curriculum is both simple and
inevitable. Learning must occur in some sequence and there
must also be some correlation between different sequences of
learning. These sequences and correlations could, of course, be
different for each individual. To some extent they must be, and
every educator pays lip service to this idea. Almost no one, on
the other hand, would insist upon avoiding all attempts to
correlate the learning programmes of different individuals.

For a teacher to impose a preferred order on his subject matter
is natural and desirable. To adjust this order to the needs of each
individual student is also desirable, but at some point may
become self-defeating. It is also desirable that teachers learn
from each other and adjust their own order of teaching accord-
ingly. But imposing upon teachers an order not of their own
choosing is undesirable, and requiring students to follow a
particular order, except in deference to a particular teacher, is
self-defeating. Only people committed to the idea of a knowledge
factory which must run on a prearranged schedule will disagree.
The argument that students and teachers must be able to transfer
from place to place without losing time is valid only if the synchronized knowledge factory is assumed.

Synchronized learning requires, however, not merely a standard order imposed on all students and teachers, but also the
integration of the different orders of the various subject matters.
This integration of curricular sequence creates the school system,
which in turn constrains individual schools in all of their major

characteristics. Thus, the core curriculum of secondary schools is dictated by standard requirements for college entrance. Since the economic value of other curricula depends upon their relationship to the core curriculum, this curriculum directly or indirectly determines hours of attendance, classroom standards, teacher qualifications and entrance requirements for the entire secondary-school system. Schools which deviate significantly from any of these norms lose their accreditation and their ability to qualify students for college entrance. Even primary-school reforms can survive only if they do not threaten the progression of their graduates through the higher reaches of the system.

It is by way of the standardized graded curriculum, therefore, that schools become a system which then acquires an international monopoly of access to jobs and to political and other social roles. It can be argued that this monopoly is not by any means complete. Some corporations will still employ the unschooled genius, while Roosevelt and Churchill did not have to pay more than lip service to the schools they attended. But these are exceptions and, if the trend continues, they will not exist for long.[4] Organization by grade, standardized intelligence and achievement testing, promotion within the system and certification for employment, are all justified by a curriculum which determines the internal structure and operations of a school, relationships between schools, and relationships between school and other institutions.

Would an educational institution lacking one of the defining characteristics proposed above still be recognizable as a school? Perhaps theoretically an institution based on children, teachers and classrooms, but without curriculum, might be called a school but it would have little resemblance to schools as we know them, and could more accurately be called a collection of training centres. Schools without children can be imagined but adults would not, for long, put up with teachers, classrooms, required attendance and curriculum. Schools for children without teachers are hard to imagine, while a child/teacher/curriculum combination appears intrinsically unstable without the restraining influence of the classroom. Teachers and children alone might work, but they would be hard to recognize as an institution, let alone a school. It is easy, on the other hand, to see children, teachers, classroom attendance and curriculum as created by and for each other. It is also easy to see schools as a stable element in a fully technological world. Schools treat people and knowledge the way a technolgical world treats everything: as if they could be processed. Anything can, of course, be processed, but only at a price, part of which involves ignoring certain aspects of the thing and certain by-products of the process. The price of processing people is intrinsically high. They tend to resist. What has to be left unprocessed may be the most important part of the person. Some of the by-products of educational processing are already evident. The greatest danger, however, lies in the prospect of success. A successfully processed humanity would lose the little control of its destiny which has always distinguished man from the rest of the world.[5]

Ritual is play: it defines our Utopias and gives expression to our dreams. Ritual is serious play, but if we believe that our ritualized Utopia is an accomplished fact, it ceases to be play and becomes an ideological instrument of oppression.

Jordan Bishop

4 How Schools Work

As the song writer said, long before Marshall McLuhan, 'It ain't what you do, it's the way that you do it'. In the case of schools the medium really *is* the message. Schooling is social ritual, bridging the gap between social theory and social practice. In psychological terms, ritual makes it possible to live with cognitive dissonance which arises from discrepancies between ideals and actions.[1] Corresponding to ideals and actions at the personal level are ideologies and practices at the level of society. To discuss schools in these terms is to ask, not what they do functionally, or what they are in essence, but how they achieve the effects on behaviour which they observably do achieve.

It may be useful to begin with an example from religion, where ritual is more familiar. The discrepancies between Christian precept and Christian practice are well known, thanks to ministers and priests. Christians are supposed to do unto others as they would have others do unto them. They are supposed to give others double what they ask. They are supposed to share all they have and to seek out those in trouble so as to minister to their needs. In practice, most nominal Christians are businessmen, professional men or workers who drive a hard bargain, look out for their own, regard the poor as shiftless and undeserving and stay as far away from prisons, slums and charity hospitals as they can. The discrepancies between teaching and practice are reconciled by participation in the rituals of church attendance, baptism, communion, prayer and Christian burial, to name but a few. There are, of course, a minority of Christians who live according to Christ's teachings. Among them are such modern martyrs as Camillo Torres and Martin Luther King, many recent victims of Brazilian torture, and many more undistinguished men and women, all over the world, fighting for justice or serving the poor.

Just how rituals serve to help people believe they are Christians, when their behaviour deviates sharply from Christian teaching, is not easy to understand. It is clear that they do, however, just as saluting the flag helps the man who cheats on income tax believe he is a first-class citizen. One explanation is that people are fallible, that their intentions matter more than their actions, and that ritual provides a means of expressing what is in their hearts. This explanation may be plausible where religion and patriotism are concerned. It will have hard going when we begin to look at schools.

Let us look at four ideologies which play a prominent role in society, examine the corresponding realities, and then identify the scholastic rituals which help to bridge the gap between ideology and reality. The ideologies selected are those which deal with equal opportunity, freedom, progress and efficiency.

There is equal opportunity, according to the ideology of modern societies, for every man to achieve whatever his ambitions dictate and his abilities permit. This ideology asserts that all levels and branches of schooling are open to all and that scholars are limited only by their dedication and brains. It proclaims that all occupations and social levels are open to anyone with enough drive and the ability to deliver the goods. Increasingly the school is recognized as the major avenue to occupations and social roles, and the openness of scholastic channels is, therefore, stressed as guaranteeing access not only to academic but to social advancement. This is the ideology of equal opportunity: pretending to make everyone's advancement depend solely upon his own personal qualities.

The reality is that all advancement is at the expense of others. Schools, occupational ladders and social class structures are all hierarchies in the shape of pyramids. In school, each higher grade is also smaller. Seldom can grades or levels be skipped. Each successive competition must be survived, therefore, in order to reach the top. In industry the picture is the same. For every president of Standard Oil, ten thousand office boys are left behind.

At what age are the opportunities equal? At birth? It seems unlikely that at birth the son of a president, even though he should begin as office boy, would have no better chance than the son of an office boy. But, if not equal at birth, the chances certainly become less equal with every year of life. By the time school begins, no one has irrevocably lost, but as soon as kindergarten is over, grades and I Q scores are recorded, and from then on the door is almost closed for those whose grades and scores are low. This is not because these grades and scores are valid. Even those who believe in them admit that at this age they are highly unreliable.[2] But judgements have to be made. Judgement about which school, which track, which teacher; all judgements that vitally influence the chances for the future. Once the elementary school is passed, it is nonsense to speak any longer of equal opportunity for those who have not done well enough to go on to a good academic secondary school. One trade-school boy in thousands may wind up as head of a construction company, but this is the great exception. In fact, every step up the ladder for one is a step down for another; one can rise to the top only over the heads of thousands. Corresponding to the ideology of equal opportunity is the reality of enforced inequality, with the odds of staying near the bottom many times higher than the odds of getting to the top.[3]

'But of course!' will be the reply. This is the nature of hierarchy. Everyone understands what equal opportunity means. If this is so, then why not tell it like it is? Call it the social lottery. In truth, it would have to be called the loaded social lottery, with each child getting as many chances as his father has dollars. But this would not suit the purposes served by calling it equal opportunity. Everyone is supposed to think he has an equal chance whether he does or not. It is better for his morale. For the moment, the question is not whether this should or should not be. This is how it is and the question is, how is it kept that way? How are people induced to believe, or at least act as though they believed, in equal opportunity when in fact there is no such thing?

They are induced to believe it by ritual progression up the ladder – the school ladder, the promotion ladder, the income ladder, the social status ladder. As long as people are climbing, it is easy to maintain the illusion that all roads lead to the top. One step at a time, that's how one gets there. The fact that there isn't enough time in a normal life-span for the man who gets to the top to touch all the steps on the way is easily overlooked. It makes sense that if you climb, step by step, you get to the top.

There are enough steps so that everyone can climb a few. Grades in school are easy enough at first, in rich countries, and almost everyone passes these early grades. By the time the going gets rough the lesson has been learned: there is equal opportunity, but men just aren't all equal. The job ladder works the same way. Everybody except those who really did badly in school gets to go up a few steps. Then the intervals get longer. People get a little older. It doesn't matter so much anymore.

Everyone's income also is allowed to rise a little, even if he doesn't get promoted. Annual increments, each year a little more; and by the time the plateau is reached the illusion is also established that everyone has had a chance. Some are just luckier than others. Obviously this is not the whole truth. But people are induced to believe it by participation in the ritual of progression.

The ideology of freedom is that all men have certain inalienable rights: the right of assembly, the right of petition for redress of grievances, the right to be free from unreasonable searches and seizures, the right to counsel, the right not to bear witness against themselves – i.e. to be free from torture in the first, second or third degrees. The facts are that all over the world the flickering lights of freedom are going out. In the communist world, deviationists and enemies of the people have no civil rights. In the capitalist world, over half of the nations which were democracies twenty years ago now have military régimes, many of which use torture as an everyday instrument of government. The remaining 'democratic' governments include South Africa, where civil rights extend only to non-Africans and non-Asians, and then only if they are careful to leave the issue of apartheid alone. In the United States there is the South, where blacks have the rights which whites deign to give them. In the rest of the country peoples' rights are increasingly determined by police and national guardsmen. Black Panthers, dissident Democrats and college students are ever more in danger of having rites instead of rights.

How is belief in freedom maintained in the face of these facts?

Largely by the rituals of democratic process. Among other things, the last presidential election in the United States helped people forget the police power used at the Chicago Convention by one wing of the Democratic Party against the other. Equally, the last national election in France helped people forget the military and police suppression of students and workers which had occurred just a few months before. These dramatic examples, however, are not as important as the daily rituals of democracy in convincing people there is freedom where there is increasing domination and suppression. The professor, exhibiting his academic freedom by denouncing the establishment, students flaunting hair styles and kicking up their bare feet, sit-ins, paint-ins, sleep-ins and pot parties – useful as these things are, they serve to reassure people that they are still free when in fact they may not be.

In the outside world, we have the angry editorial, the enterprising reporter's exposé, the new magazine going the old ones one better, the legislative investigation. A few serve good purposes. Many more merely help to maintain the illusion of freedom. These examples are deliberately chosen not to represent pure ritual. Whether the acts cited above are real or ritual depends on who is doing what for what purpose. Ritual plays a positive as well as a negative role in human affairs. The fact that the rituals of freedom are equivocal testifies to the duality of ritual as well as to the subtleties of freedom. With few exceptions, only those who know how to play the game – those already in positions of privilege – even though dissident, are able to use the liberty which democratic process provides. Those who are truly deprived have little real access to democratic process. This is one reason Jefferson despaired of orderly reform, carried out within the rules. But the rules themselves, ritually followed, disguise the basis for Jefferson's reliance on periodic revolution. The democratic process, in school and society, helps people accept the discrepancy between the assumption of freedom and the facts of domination and suppression. We do not want to lose our democratic process but neither do we want to delude ourselves about how much freedom we have. We can extend the limits of our own and other people's freedom only if we know what obstacles stand in the way.

The ideology of progress is that our situation is improving and will continue to improve, without any demonstrable limits upon the degree or scope of future improvements. The facts are that we are near the limits at which the atmosphere can absorb more heat or the seas more pollution, near the limits of the earth to support more population, near the limits of the patience of the poor to subsist on the bounty of the rich, near the limits of the rich themselves to either tighten further the screws they have fastened on themselves or to live much longer with the indulgences they have invented. People who do not want to face the implications of these facts say that the problems they imply will be solved by new discoveries and inventions. But the discoveries and inventions of the past have merely brought us to our present predicament. Future discoveries and inventions can only sharpen this predicament. For regardless of how near or far away the limits are there can be little doubt that they exist, while the ideology of progress knows no limits. The earth, human population and human nature are all finite while progress is infinite. This theoretical problem might not have to bother people if various kinds of progress were in reasonable balance, but this is not the case. Our ability to kill each other and ourselves is growing much faster than our productive capacity. The gap between the rich and the poor is rapidly widening. Psychological tensions are increasing much faster than our ability to deal with them.

The ideology of progress is, then, faced with a set of very hard facts which contradict its assumptions. How are these contradictions reconciled? They are kept from consciousness primarily by the ritual of research – the continuing quest for new knowledge, new insights, new techniques. Research is a very important non-ritual fact, but it is also an important ritual. The ritual of research induces the belief that new discoveries change the whole picture, that every day is a new day with a new set of rules and possibilities. This is clearly false. Even the most important new discoveries and inventions leave almost everything else unchanged. The invention of breeder reactors stretched the world's supply of fissionable material enormously. Nuclear fission extends the limits of possible energy sources even more. But these far-reaching developments do not affect the absorption capacity of the atmosphere at all. They have no effect on human population except to threaten its total annihilation. They influence man's ability to think and to govern himself in only the slightest degree. Yet the myth of renewal by research, the belief that major new discoveries can renew all terms of all problems – this myth and belief permit men to avoid seeing the very hard barriers to further progress which in fact exist.

Research is so identified with school that its impact as ritual renewal affects students even more than it does the general population. The greatest impact of research on students, however, comes by way of its effects on curriculum. One of the hallmarks of modern schooling, which separates it most sharply from its own tradition, is that its offerings are labelled as ever new. Yesterday's knowledge is out of date. In Norway serious thought is being given to declaring degrees more than five years old invalid. The merit of this proposal is that it belatedly recognizes what was always true, that degrees have little validity. Its rationale, however, is that five-year-old knowledge is no longer valid. Every worker is obliged to come back periodically to the school to refurbish the knowledge he received the last time. Real education is, of course, a life-time process. But real education and real research are also continuous, not periodic processes. Genuine research and education integrate the new into the much greater mass of the old, and this can only be done in the course of work, in the actual discovery and application of the new. The ritual of renewal does serve its purpose, the purpose of re-creation, which need not be superficial. When it clothes the nakedness of the myth of progress, however, it does a great disservice. And this it does particularly by way of the school. The illusion that knowledge must be contemporary to be valid stands between the generations. This conceit of the young is largely the result of the ritual of curriculum renewal as practised by the school.[4]

The ideology of efficiency is that modern man has solved his production problems by means of efficient organization, that other men can do likewise, and that most of man's remaining problems can be solved by a similar approach. The fact is, as Kenneth Boulding has recently suggested, that gross national product, the current measure of a nation's output, is actually a measure of economic inefficiency. Employment in the wealthier countries increasingly follows Parkinson's law – that employment increases as production decreases. More and more people in the wealthier countries are employed in the service sector, doing things of dubious value. Consider government and corporate bureaucrats, salesmen, advertisers, bankers, accountants, lawyers, teachers, policemen, soldiers, poll-takers, social workers, for example. There is no doubt that all of these people do something that someone values, but there is also little doubt that as many people hate what they do. Lawyers provide the clearest example; for every winner at law there is a loser. The same thing holds, a little less obviously, for all of the kinds of workers listed above and for many other services as well. Many physical goods are also of dubious value. Military weapons, pornography and billboards certainly have as many detractors as supporters. Super-jets, automobiles, gravestones and schools are also in the doubtful category. Meat products, tobacco, alcohol, marijuana and fluoridated water all have varying degrees of opposition. The point is not that work is bad or even, in itself, of doubtful value. It is rather that the value of work depends upon what it produces.

Most people would agree that efficiency is misapplied to killing, loving and eating, for example. But the ideology of efficiency does not reflect these reservations. Its high priests have no qualms about drugging children to keep them quiet in school, using electro-shock to torture prisoners or napalm to burn Vietnamese villages. How, then, are the discrepancies between the ideology and the facts of efficiency kept from overwhelming the public conscience? The answer is that it is done through the ritual of activity.

Schools learned long ago that the way to keep children from thinking is to keep them busy. Classes, clubs, athletics, cultural activities, homework; the devil finds work for idle hands to do. This is also how attacks on the efficiency of the school are met – more courses, more degrees, more activities, more enrolment. The graduates of school are well prepared to participate in the activity rites of the outside world: more committees, more projects, more campaigns, more products, more industries, more employment, more gross national product. Not all activity is ritual. But in a nation capable of producing all of its agricultural and industrial products with 5 per cent of its labour force, as is the United States (see page 63), ritual must account for much of the remaining 95 per cent. It must also account for much of the time of adults who are not in the labour force and of students who are in school.

Schools have succeeded in ritualizing education because they serve societies which dedicate themselves to consumption, which assume that man wants principally to consume and that in order to consume endlessly he must bind himself to the wheel of endless production. The whole theory of schooling is based on the assumption that production methods applied to learning will result in learning. They do result in learning how to produce and consume – so long as nothing fundamental changes. As a means of learning to adapt to changing circumstances, production methods are ridiculous. The need to distinguish these two kinds of learning is kept from our attention mainly by our participation in the scholastic ritual.

A single shelf of a good European library was worth the whole native literature of India and Arabia.... It is, I believe, no exaggeration to say that all the historical information which has been collected from all the books written in the Sanskrit language is less valuable than what may be found in the most paltry abridgements used at preparatory schools in England.... I think it clear that ... neither as the languages of the law nor as the languages of religion, have the Sanskrit and Arabic any peculiar claim to our engagement, that it is possible to make natives of this country thoroughly good English scholars and that to this end our efforts ought to be directed.... We must at present do our best to form a class who may be interpreters between us and the millions whom we govern, a class of persons Indian in blood and colour, but English in taste, in opinions, in morals and in intellect.

Lord Macaulay: Parliamentary minute on Indian education

5 Where Schools Came From

School is a stage in a succession of specialized institutions. Prehistoric rites, myths and shamans, temples and priestly castes, Sumerian, Grecian, Alexandrian and Roman schools, monastic orders, early universities, common and grammar schools – all have played a part in the history of the national and international school system of today. Counterparts can be found for the functions and elements of modern schools at each stage of this history. Comparisons which span millenia run the risk of distorting meanings, but this risk is worth taking in order to learn from the educational trends and inventions of the past. One of the most general and instructive trends is the progressive specialization of content, method, personnel and location in something which was originally much more than education and which, in schooling, has become something much less.

Since 1820 archaeology and anthropology have extended the history of man many tens of thousands of years.[1] As far back as the record goes, man has engaged in specialized activities which have important things in common with what goes on in schools. Rites and rituals – symbolic practices seemingly unnecessary to the satisfaction of elementary physical needs – have always been part of man's repertoire. In this man is not unique; animals engage in similar practices which seem to serve no elementary function, and even sometimes to harm the individual or the species. As far back as man's record goes, we also find evidence of people and places specialized in and for the use of myth and ritual. Some of the earliest records are in just such places: the caves of southern France and Spain, famous for their paintings of prehistoric animals, were apparently used largely for ritual practices. The only human figures included in the paintings are those of shamans, who combined the teacher's role with that of priest, magician, actor, artist, poet and ideologue. These, at any rate, are roles combined in shamans of existing tribes, whose technology and art resemble those of prehistoric man.

Reasoning both from archaeological and modern anthropological evidence, it appears that prehistoric rites shared certain elements of current curricula. They had an age-specific character, acting out the myths related to birth, adolescence and death. They explained and celebrated both the everyday and the unusual aspects of the world. They provided activity for idle periods that followed hunt or harvest. They allowed young people to try on adult roles for size.

The line between prehistoric and historic time is marked by the invention of writing, which corresponds roughly in time to the establishment of cities and the great religions. Education emerged out of the practice of worship and government. Its early home was the temple-court and its early practitioners were specialized priests. Writing itself was probably invented by such specialists. Shamans and priests are, thus, in the central line not only of the development of teachers and schools but of the evolution of man. Brain, hand and tongue; horde, village and city; magic, religion, art and science – these are the milestones of man's physical, social and spiritual development. The priesthoods of city-based religions inherited from their country-cousin shamans a mixture of magic, religion, art and science which they began to disentangle and specialize. It is relatively well established that not only writing but accounting and mathematics, astronomy and chemistry, music, painting and poetry had their early development in the temple-courts of Egyptian, Sumerian and other ruling castes, which combined the functions of priest and king.[2] The first formalized teaching of these arts, which still make up most of the modern core-curriculum, must have been a master–apprentice type of teaching. Even earlier, a kind of teaching among equals must have occurred, as one individual shared his discoveries or developments with others. Here is one of the two main roots of the modern school, at the very origin of systematic knowledge. This root does not appear again, in an institutionally prominent form, until the rise of the universities of the Middle Ages.

The other, much humbler, root makes its first appearance in a Sumerian classroom built to accommodate about thirty children, the discovery of which led to the speculation that modern modal class-size may have been based on the limitations of Sumerian brick and architecture.[3]

Plato and Aristophanes were the first to leave surviving written records of classroom and school.[4,5] These first schools of classical Athens were humble indeed – mere appendages to an educational programme which stressed military training, athletics, music and poetry, and which taught reading, writing and arithmetic almost as an afterthought. Originally all education in Athens was tutorial – one aspect of personal relationships which were often erotic as well. As Athens became more democratic, and pupils began to outnumber masters, group instruction gradually replaced the tutorial relationships.

Soon after the first reference in Greek writing to group instruction in literary arts and skills, schools of medicine and philosophy are also mentioned and, soon afterwards, a class of schools conducted by Sophist philosophers.[6] These first models of intermediate schools were based on contracts between a master and a group of parents for the instruction of their sons during a three or four year period of their adolescence. The Sophists were the first paid teachers on record, and their aim, appropriately, was practical: to make of their students successful men of affairs.

From these meagre beginnings in the golden age of Greece, there flourished in the hellenistic colonies scattered by the conquests of Alexander all over the ancient world school systems prophetic of our own in organization, curriculum and the age-span of students. Children first learned reading, writing and numbers, and later were taught gymnastics, music, the classics of literature, geometry and science. The museums of Alexandria and other cities specialized in the teaching of medicine, rhetoric and philosophy. Most of these centres, patronized largely by Greek families, were privately financed, although a few small cities had public systems while others were supported by foundations established by wealthy men. One of the main purposes of these schools was to keep alive the hellenic tradition in a barbarian world. Only a small minority of the Greek population of the Alexandrian world was ever able to take full advantage of them.

The Romans adopted the hellenistic school and, with minor modifications, used it for the education of their own élite. From the fall of Athens to the fall of Byzantium, therefore, a tiny minority of the world's population was schooled in somewhat the fashion of today. The school was not, however, an important institution in Graeco-Roman or in Byzantine times except for its role in preserving the memory and some of the culture of ancient Greece until the time of the Renaissance in western Europe.

Except in Byzantium, the fall of Rome resulted in a reunion of education and religion which lasted for a thousand years. The educational institutions of the Middle Ages were the cathedral schools and the monasteries. More specialized in their purpose than the ancient temples, they also had a more limited educational role; they did, nevertheless, introduce a number of important ideas into the history of western education. In the earliest Benedictine monasteries, space and time became the parameters of learning as well as of living.[7] Every hour of Benedictine life had its appointed place and task. Adherence to this regimen constituted the good life; no external product or other sign presumed to attest the efficacy of the life thus lived.

The subsequent Dominican and Franciscan orders were based on different principles. Dependence upon the charity of others and identification with the poor replaced the bondage of time and space.[8,9] As in the case of the Benedictine rituals, begging and the care of the sick and destitute were not designed as training for subsequent living but as a way of life.

The preparatory principle of education was revived by the Jesuits, who in the sixteenth century extended and rationalized schooling well beyond the limits of Graeco-Roman times.[10] The ancient schools had never been more than a small part of an educational programme which was a product of tradition rather than of rational forethought. The Jesuits developed a curriculum and an educational method deliberately designed to prepare men not merely for an ordinary life but for a life of unprecedented scope and challenge. At least part of the subsequent growth of schooling is undoubtedly due to their initial brilliant successes.

Originally intended for members of an élite religious order,

Jesuit schooling was soon extended to the lay élites of the European medieval world. The rate of this extension and the circumstances under which it occurred are strongly reminiscent of the sudden growth of Greek schooling following the conquest of Alexander. It was the insecurity rather than the dominance of the Greek colonies of Alexandrian times which caused them to build and depend upon schools; it was the insecurity of the Roman church in the time of Ignatius which accounts for the formation and rapid growth of the Jesuit system of schools. In both cases, the school was seen as a way of preserving a set of values which were losing their dominance.

This chronology of the Christian orders has run ahead of at least one major event in the history of schooling – the foundation of the first medieval universities.[11] Originally devoted primarily to the study of Christian theology, they quickly branched into other fields of knowledge and, long before the Reformation, had become independent institutions in so far as this was possible in medieval Europe. Along with their counterparts in the Moslem world, the universities of Bologna, Salerno and Paris became the first institutions of any size devoted primarily to the development and propagation of knowledge. They were also, of course, the direct predecessors of modern universities, and thus of the upper layer of the present school system.

Luther and his followers, coinciding so neatly in time with Gutenberg's invention of movable type, gave a vast stimulus to the growth of the lower schools in northern Europe. The large-scale printing of bibles, and the doctrine that salvation was directly derivable from them, made the teaching of reading a moral imperative for Protestants who could afford it. The industrial revolution, coming so closely on the heels of the Reformation, supplied the last condition necessary for the rapid proliferation of schools, providing not only the means, but also a secular rationale for widespread literacy.[12]

Mere growth in the number of schools did not result in school systems. This dimension of schooling came with the development of the nation state. Thus, while public schools first burgeoned in the federated United States, the first integrated systems of schooling developed in France and Prussia. The Prussian development, although later, was the more clear cut and became an important international model. In Prussia and later in Germany, the development of the school system was coterminous with the development of the nation state and was deliberately designed to be one of its principal pedestals.[13]

One aspect of the German school system was the teaching of high German, the language of the school and the unifying language of the state. A common, graded, integrated curriculum was another – designed to serve the military, political and manpower needs of the nation. A hierarchically organized teaching profession was still another. Most important of all was a carefully thought out philosophy of education, reflected in school organization, logistics, curriculum, teacher recruitment, teaching methods and scholastic ritual, and aimed at producing a citizenry tailored to the specifications of the architects of the German nation state. No other national system has been so systematically designed. But all nations, in copying to a greater or lesser degree the major features of the German system, have in effect adopted its objectives and its methods. England has perhaps copied them least, but even England's former colonies have followed Germany more than England.

In France the idea of a national school system first arose partly in opposition to the Jesuits who, in the sixteenth century, were among the principal educators of the élites.[14] Despite the suppression of the order in 1763, and the attempts of the legislators of the French Revolution, public schools made little headway. After the restoration of the Monarchy the Jesuits and, at the primary level, the Christian Brothers again played an important role in French education. The educational reform law of 1834 called for friendly relations between church and state, but the resulting collaboration did not survive the crisis created by the French defeat in 1870.[15] The power of Prussian arms was attributed by many to the efficiency of their national school system and no effort was spared to initiate a similar system in France.

Public schools in the United States have also had a long and complicated history. Despite the early establishment of public schools in New England, Pennsylvania and Virginia, these schools remained for a long time under local control and, except in New England, the privilege of a relatively small minority.[16,17]

The original New England schools were quasi-universal, without being compulsory, because their promoters shared a common conception of man, God and the world. Even in New England, public schooling became much less than universal with the influx of non-Puritan immigrants beginning early in the nineteenth century. It was, in fact, this lapse from a brief tradition of universal schooling that led Horace Mann to formulate the modern American concept of the public school.[18]

Mann's public schools required attendance because persons of different origins, values and faiths had to be brought to share a common conception which the Pilgrims had taken for granted. These two approaches to universal public schooling illustrate the contradictions which have brought a glorious promise to a dismal end. Thomas Jefferson,[19] Orestes Brownson[20] and John Dewey[21] saw universal education as the means of equipping men to discover their beliefs and to create their institutions. St Ignatius of Loyola, Johann Gottlieb Fichte and Horace Mann saw a similar process as the means of shaping men to the requirements of social goals and institutions assumed to have prior validity.

These ideological strains combined to make public schools popular with both the privileged and the deprived. For the latter, they held the promise of equal opportunity; for the former, the promise of orderly progression under control of the élite. To a degree, both promises were realized, but the contradictions inherent in them have become steadily more obvious as the balance of power has shifted from citizens to the state. In their time, Locke and Jefferson prevailed. John Dewey's more recent effort to put man back in the saddle was merely given lip service.

The organizational, legal and procedural steps which have welded tens of thousands of nominally independent local school districts and thousands of colleges and universities into a national school system are the logical outcome of a philosophy which views schools as serving national ends.

The popularity of such a philosophy, in a century which has seen the number of nations in the world more than tripled, is not surprising. The proliferation of nation states is clearly one of the major factors in the growth of the international school system. Regardless of reasons, however, the actual development of such a system is one of the amazing facts of human history. Schools are, of course, only one of the technological institutions which have spread from Europe and North America over the rest of the world; but all of the others are more easily explained, while none has spread like schooling. Universal schooling has become part of the official programme of almost every nation. Every state must have its university, every city its high school, every hamlet its primary school. All nations look to the leading nations for models of curriculum, scholastic organization and scholastic standards. Capitalist and communist nations compete in schooling their populations, with as little argument about the standards of competition as in the Olympics.

How is all this to be explained? Technology, the profit motive and the world struggle for power explain most of the growth of international institutions. None of them directly explains the case of schooling. Similarity of constitutions and codes of law can in some cases be explained as the residue of empire and in others as ideological emulation. The spread of hospitals and medical technology can be attributed to the demonstrated efficacy of at least some aspects of modern medicine. There is nothing comparable in modern schooling; schools are as free of the obligation to justify themselves as were the Benedictine monasteries.

European world domination during the eighteenth and nineteenth centuries helps to explain the existence of school systems in former colonies. Japanese schools can also be explained in part as a colonial phenomenon, developed as part of a general western pattern and adopted to avoid colonization. Schools have clearly lagged the most in those parts of the world least influenced by European and American industrialization.

Schools have served a major purpose in the consolidation of the new nation states which grew out of the wreckage of empire. They also serve the élites of these new nations, providing access to international politics, economics and culture. This does not, however, explain the international popularity of mass education. The real explanation can be traced back to the two previous historic explosions of schooling, the Alexandrian and the Jesuit. As noted, both of these occurred at times when traditional value systems were in jeopardy. This is again the case, but this time the values involved are more basic and more universal than those of Hellas or medieval Europe. In question now are the assumptions of a society based on hierarchy of privilege. The technology which invalidates these assumptions has created the antidote for its own effects: a school system which promises access to the goods of technology but denies it in fact.

Modern technology relieves man, for the first time in history, of the need to earn his bread by the sweat of his brow. All pre-industrial societies required close to 80 per cent of the labour force to be engaged in agriculture. Now, using existing techniques, 5 per cent of the labour force of a modern society could produce all of the agricultural and industrial goods currently consumed.

Even now, 10 per cent of the labour force of the United States produces 90 per cent of its agricultural and industrial output. And this is almost entirely prior to the application of existing methods of automation, and in the face of widespread job-protective pressures from organized labour. Nevertheless, the United States is producing record agricultural surpluses while paying farmers billions of dollars to restrict production. Additional billions of dollars of industrial goods are being produced for commercial export, over and above the value of goods imported. A huge bill of military goods is being produced while massive space and research programmes are under way. If labour and management could agree upon the objective, 5 per cent of the United States labour force could within a very few years produce the goods currently being consumed by the domestic civilian population. This bill of goods, although badly distributed, leaving many people deprived, is nevertheless enormously wasteful in its average composition. It provides an excessive and otherwise unhealthful diet, clothing which is discarded because of style changes rather than wear, so-called durable goods which are made to wear out in a few years, a tremendous packaging component which merely multiplies the pollution problem, and an unbelievable quantity of junk which serves only to relieve the boredom of people whose lives, devoted to the consumption and production of goods and services, have been emptied of real meaning. We would live much better on half as much. Such a society does not require a hierarchy of privilege for any of the reasons which have justified such a hierarchy in the past. Modern institutions have assumed the burden of maintaining and justifying a continuing hierarchy of privilege. Among these institutions, school plays a central role. School qualifies men for participation in other institutions and convicts those who do not meet its requirements of not deserving desirable roles in these institutions.

In less than a hundred years industrial society has moulded patent solutions to basic human needs and converted us to the belief that man's needs were shaped by the Creator as demands for the products we have invented. This is as true for Russia and Japan as for the North Atlantic community. The consumer is trained for obsolescence, which means continuing loyalty toward the same producers who will give him the same basic packages in different quality or new wrappings.

Industrialized societies can provide such packages for personal consumption for most of their citizens, but this is no proof that these societies are sane, or economical, or that they promote life. The contrary is true. The more the citizen is trained in the consumption of packaged goods and services, the less effective he seems to be in shaping his environment. His energies and finances are consumed in procuring ever new models of his staples, and the environment becomes a by-product of his own consumption habits.

Ivan Illich: *Celebration of Awareness*

6 Institutional Props for Privilege

Schools are not the only institutions which promise the world and then become the instruments of its denial. This is what churches, to give one plural label to all religious institutions, have always done: packaged the free gift of God, or nature so that a price could be exacted for it, and then withheld it from people unable or unwilling to pay the price. Churches were remarkable among other institutions, until recently, only for their hypocrisy. Other traditional institutions never pretended to offer a universal gift. Even the prehistoric practitioners of religious magic did not do so. It is the unique mark of the great religions that their founders opened the doors of the spirit to all and that their priests then succeeded in holding these doors open with one hand while charging admission with the other.

Except for churches, traditional institutions were always openly run for the benefit of those who ran them. Courts, kingdoms, armies, empires and enterprises belonged to their possessors and shared their benefits only with a few and only for a fee. Two non-religious institutions have recently begun to make the claim of offering universal access: first, nation states and their sub-systems such as schools and, second, modern production enterprises.

Something for nothing is not the issue. No religious leader has ever promised something for nothing, but only that the door would open to all those who would follow the path. This is the promise which churches have reneged on, in failing to keep their own doors open, and which many modern enterprises and public bureaucracies falsely proclaim. They do more. They take elaborate and effective steps, first to sell their promise, and then to frustrate its fulfilment.

As provision for human needs is institutionalized, the in-

stitutions in question define a product and control access to it.
They progressively:

1. Define the product or service which satisfies the need (e.g.
schools define education as schooling).

2. Induce general acceptance of this definition among the needy
(e.g. people are persuaded to identify education as schooling).

3. Exclude part of the needy population from full access to the
product or service (e.g. schools, at some level, are available to
only some people).

4. Pre-empt the resources available for satisfying the need (e.g.
schools use up the resources available for education).

The above generalizations hold for health, transportation and
many other kinds of human needs, as well as for education.

Health is progressively defined and conceived as access to the
services of physicians and hospitals and to the products of the
drug industry. This access is notoriously unequal. The cost of
hospitals, doctors and drugs is increasing faster than the resources available to pay for them. It can also be argued that the
health of mature populations, those whose birth and death rates
are converging, is getting worse as expenditures for hospitals,
doctors and drugs increase. This is to say that we are achieving
a longer sick-life by means of these expenditures. People may
indulge themselves more as more remedies become available,
but if more resources were devoted to preventive measures, sickness as well as death rates would decline.

In the case of transportation, the facts are even clearer. The
private automobile has almost displaced its competitors in many
countries. In the United States, saturation is reaching the point
of declining utility, even for car owners, yet half the adult
population remains without dependable access to a private car
and has a harder time getting transportation than if cars had
never been invented. Even in Los Angeles, which reputedly has
more cars than people, and which is drowning in its own exhaust, there are as many old and young people who cannot or are
not allowed to drive as there are qualified drivers.[1] These people,
even those who belong to families which include qualified driv-

ers, must wait upon the convenience of their chauffeurs, or vice versa.

Provision for a category of human need is institutionalized to the extent that there is a prevailing standard product or service, a standard production and distribution process, and a standard price (with the concept of price including all significant conditions of access). It is worth noting that the people priced out of the market are convinced not only of their unworthiness to participate in it, e.g. their inability to pursue college studies or to wear stylish clothes, but also of their unworthiness to participate in the privileges which college education and stylish clothes imply.

Until democracy was popularized and technology institutionalized, claims of universal political and economic participation could not be made. Now such claims sound plausible and are widely believed. The makers of these claims come with specific products designed to meet specific needs. They elaborate a package which becomes ever more complex, more exclusive of access and more expensive. More basic, however, than product elaboration is the identification of need with product. The words education and school, health and hospital, transportation and automobile, become inseparable. People forget that there were educated men before there were schools, healthy men before there were hospitals, and that men walked and rode before they drove or flew

As institutions grow, more and more people accept the identification of need and product. Only the Jews and the Moors of medieval Europe failed to identify salvation with the Catholic Church. Women, who throughout history have borne their babies in the fields, are now recruited into maternity wards. Peasants who have never seen schools vote for the candidates who promise them.

The elaboration process effectively prevents the realization of these promises, even for the simplest products. Pins and needles can be packaged in ever fancier collections. Salt can be made a monopoly product and a form of tax. One of Ghandi's first struggles in India was against the salt monopoly maintained by the British Government.[2] The Italian Government still maintains a monopoly on salt except in Sicily, where salt is produced. What happens to schools, hospitals and automobiles is common knowledge. People are priced out of the market not only directly but by increasingly complicated rules – drivers' licenses, entrance examinations, insurance requirements. There are good reasons for all the rules but their proliferation tends to shrink the proportion of qualified consumers.

There are, of course, opposing processes. Because of consumer credit, rising incomes, growth of public systems of schools and hospitals, etc., net access to modern institutions may even gradually increase. Beyond question, however, the excluded portion of the population, even if declining in number, gets steadily worse off as the monopoly of an institutional product is established. No resources remain for alternative products. As school budgets grow, support for educational alternatives must decline. Not only do school dropouts find progressively less educational resources, they also have less job opportunities. And, finally, they have less excuses. As automobiles increase in number, there are less trains and buses; those which survive are more expensive, less satisfactory and less profitable.[3] The number of new owners of automobiles increased by no more than twenty-five million during the past decade. Perhaps a roughly equivalent number enjoyed for the first time the benefits of modern medical services other than inoculation. The number of school children may have increased by a hundred million. But the population of the world increased by almost a billion during the decade, so that the numbers without any of these services increased vastly more than the numbers with them. Even more were priced out of the market during this period. The price of automobiles increased substantially, while the cost of medical services and schools multiplied several times. Meanwhile, *per capita* income, on a world-wide basis, rose very little. Even if there had been no population growth and other things had remained equal, more people would have been priced out of the markets for modern goods and services during the 1960s than were added to them.

Nor can the above figures be written off by labelling the sixties as a bad decade, in which major institutions did not function as they are supposed to. In a world dominated by competition for privilege, there is no other way that institutions can function. The already privileged continue to demand better schools, better hospitals, better cars. As the number who enjoy these commodities increases, there are ever more people to be supplied with ever more expensive packages, making it increasingly difficult to extend this privilege to an ever widening ring of an ever growing population. Even without population growth, the above factors – plus ecological limits – might make it impossible ever to universalize even current standards of living in Europe and America.

The excluded are not the only, perhaps not even the principal, sufferers. Those who participate, but to a limited degree, feel sharper pain. Imagine the anguish of pious folk whose relatives languished in purgatory while those of more fortunate neighbours were professionally prayed into heaven. Imagine the torment, today, of persons whose relatives die because donors of kidneys and hearts are coopted by those who can pay. The fortunate feel no pain but they may be hurt worst of all, for they get hooked on a game which has no end and which no one can win. The struggle of the rich against old age and death is a grotesque example. Much worse, if less macabre, is the status scramble which, as it spreads to more products and more people, poisons the air, the water and the earth and sucks the very meaning out of life. A squirrel in a rotating cage is no more hopeless nor ludicrous than the Smiths and the Joneses trying to keep up with each other.

When Veblen wrote his account of conspicuous consumption fifty years ago, it was part of a theory of the leisure class.[4] Confined to this class, competitive consumption may have been morally offensive but remained socially tolerable. Extended to the masses, competitive consumption destroys man, his society and his environment. A limited leisure class could consume at the expense of the masses. Open-ended consumption can occur only at the cost of the consumer. But man can no more live in a squirrel cage than can a squirrel. Society cannot survive class conflict stoked to increasing heat by international warfare, universal advertising and competitive schooling. The world cannot absorb the waste it now receives, let alone the amount implied by present trends.

One critically important aspect of the competitive consumption of institutionalized products is competition among nations. The early products of modern institutions – people as well as things and services – were exported from Europe to the New World and to European colonies, thus providing opportunities for all members of the populations of these European nations. Those who could not attend the new schools or buy the new goods could migrate to the New World, be drafted as soldiers to police the colonies, or take over the land of those who left. They were, therefore, priced out of the new markets only temporarily. The sons of these conquerers of new lands became, in fact, the pioneers of new levels and types of human consumption.[5] The presently developing nations are not, with some exceptions, able to displace or conquer weaker peoples. Far from being able to involve their total populations in export trade, migration or conquest, they are instead required to compete inside their domestic markets with imports of foreign products, including manpower. Far more of the population of underdeveloped nations, compared with those which developed earlier, is priced out of schools, hospitals and modern transportation. This part of the population is progressively alienated from the élite of its own nation, from those who do have access to the products of modern institutions, foreign or indigenous. The alienated masses become, in turn, a demographic drag, an economic liability and, ultimately, a political opposition.[6]

This has failed to occur only in areas where development has progressed very rapidly, with correspondingly heavy imports of foreign capital and manpower. Israel, Puerto Rico and Taiwan – significantly, all very small – are the only unequivocal examples. In these areas war, migration and strategic location, respectively, have made it possible to engage the entire population in the development process, thus avoiding the social split and alienation of the non-participating element. These exceptions, therefore, prove the rule – unless it can be shown that all nations would accept similar relationships with the developed world, and that comparable rates of foreign investment could be achieved on a world-wide scale.[7]

Japan and the communist nations are special cases. The latter, by taking over the pricing mechanism, were able to force their total populations into their institutions. By doing so, they succeeded in avoiding the dilemmas of the Third World, but the procrustean character of their instutitional frameworks and the attendant difficulties are well known. These difficulties resulted, in considerable part, from the wholesale adoption of pre-communist institutions, unadapted to the purposes they were supposed to serve. By *fiat*, these institutions involved the whole population, but not in ways which resulted in high levels of motivation for socially constructive activity.

Japan's ability to maintain the character of her traditional social structure gave her a less costly means than that of the communist states. Employers were responsible for employment security and employees were willing to accept the wages offered.[8] But Japan also shared the advantages of the nations which pioneered economic development, in that she enjoyed a substantial political and economic empire which permitted her to export goods, services and manpower.

Most institutions continued to serve the interests of their inventors and, at the same time, the interests of those who were originally peripheral to them, only at the cost of an even more peripheral group.

In the days when political empires were the salient institutions, the above statement would have excited no interest. The privileges of Roman citizenship were extended only as additional territories were conquered. Marx applied the principle to capitalist institutions. We merely generalize the principle to other institutions and, possibly, free it of dependence on the notion of deliberate exploitation. Most of those attempting to universalize schooling and hospital care sincerely believe that they act in the interest of the as yet unschooled and uncured. Earlier missionaries, conquerers and even traders frequently acted with the same conviction.

What this means for development strategy is that developing nations must invent their own institutions. Obviously, these institutions must be able to use foreign components – machinery, materials, techniques, knowledge, even trained manpower. What must be indigenous are the basic institutions which determine who gets what, when, and at what price. They must not only be indigenous, however, but also new. The church and the *hacienda* will obviously not do, since they originally opened the door to foreign institutions. The feudal plantations of north-east Brazil, for example, originally provided a role, however humble, for the inhabitants of that area.[9] The importation of modern machinery reduced the demand for labour, while the importation of modern drugs increased its supply to the point where the masses of this region are now starving. A return to the *hacienda* would merely accelerate the current rate of starvation.

What must be new and indigenous are the institutional patterns, which determine how major classes of needs will be satisfied; how people will be fed, clothed, sheltered, educated, and protected from danger, disease, misfortune and exploitation.[10] Much of the technology of the modern world will be required, but it will have to be applied in a way which meets the needs of the needy.

This is impossible within the framework of the institutions of the developed world. Using the same institutions, the Third World could never catch up. The educationally more advanced nations must forever remain better educated if schools are to be the means of education. And Brazil, spending fifty dollars per student per year, can never have the schools which in North America cost a thousand dollars. Transportation can never catch up unless the less-developed nation installs more efficient factories than the developed nation. But seldom can the less-developed nation install a factory even nearly as good. If this is done in a particular case, major and expensive components must be bought from the developed nation at a price which forces this case to be an exception. The follower must, therefore, not only remain behind but fall further behind as long as he adopts the means of development of the leader.

The underdeveloped society requires more efficient institutions than those of the developed: more food, clothing, shelter, learning and protection per unit of input than modern agriculture, manufacture, construction, schooling, etc. can supply. This is possible only by departing from different premises. India may never be able to produce the US diet, but only the producers of Coca-Cola, Scotch whisky, corn-fed beef and the doctors and dentists who live on the consumers thereof really benefit from this diet. Better clothing, shelter, education and protection than the standard products of the Atlantic community are no more difficult to design than is a superior diet. Neither is there great difficulty in designing better means of producing these goods and services than the ones now in vogue.

The difficulty is that we are the prisoners of our institutions rather than their masters. Seldom do we consciously design them and, when we do, we can scarcely finish the process before bowing down in reverence. So in their thrall are we that we tremble lest we lose them inadvertently and fall helplessly back into barbarism. Actually, this fear is largely confined to the privileged, and what we really fear is that the specific bases of our own privilege might get lost in the institutional shuffle.

There is, then, a political as well as psychological aspect of the difficulty. There are those who benefit from present institutions and who consciously desire to preserve them. Among these are owners, managers, political leaders and other holders of power. But many with power have no conscious desire to monopolize it, and many over whom power is wielded give in to the illusion rather than the reality of power. Man cannot free himself from existing institutions without struggle, but neither will struggle avail unless preceded by imagination and invention. One of the major problems is that the developed nations now have an effective, if not necessarily deliberate, monopoly of the means of modern invention.

Theories of political revolution are not sufficient. Such theories assume that if a new class gains control, the society will change in accordance with the values of this class as expressed in its ideology. In practice, we see that a spate of revolutions throughout this century has left most of the specialized institutions which compose societies intact. The schools and hospitals of communist states are no different from those of capitalist states. Even the recent revolution in Cuba is attempting to extend health and education services to the masses largely by means of traditional school and hospital systems. The agricultural and industrial institutions of communist and capitalist states tend to converge, despite great efforts on both sides to make them different. According to prevailing theory, technology provides the force which defeats these efforts, but technology scarcely explains the case of the school, of the church, of the family, or of many other institutions which have, temporarily at least, defeated the efforts of revolutionary governments to change them.

Yet there is ample evidence that institutions are by no means eternal. During this century monarchies have disappeared, political empires have broken up, churches have lost their power if not their membership, labour unions have risen and declined, entrepreneurs have been replaced by managers and technicians, major industries have disappeared and been born. Many of these changes are almost totally unexplained; others, especially the political changes, have resulted from specific plans, sometimes based on a general theory of political revolution. Man has shown himself capable of creating and destroying institutions, on a planned and unplanned basis, with or without theory. At the same time, he remains the prisoner of his institutions to an almost unimaginable degree. He can break his thralldom only by first understanding it thoroughly, and then by deliberately planning the renovation and replacement of his present institutional structures. Both understanding and effective action will require a general theory encompassing a set of specific sub-theories applicable to each major type of institution.

We must develop conceptual tools for the analysis of major institutions, in order to understand the historical process by which they were introduced, the sociological process by which they became acceptable, and the limitations which they now place on the search for alternatives (not only limitations of power and resources, but also limitations upon the creative imagination). We must develop a language in which we can speak with precision about the needs of modern man – a language freed from the one which is shaped by those institutions men have come to accept as the suppliers of their specific demands.

If we continue to believe that the goals of the industrial system – the expansion of output, the companion increase in consumption, technological advance, the public images that sustain it – are coordinate with life, then all of our lives will be in the service of these goals. What is consistent with these ends we shall have or be allowed; all else will be off limits. Our wants will be managed in accordance with the needs of the industrial system; the policies of the state will be subject to similar influence; education will be adapted to industrial need; the disciplines required by the industrial system will be the conventional morality of the community. All other goals will be made to seem precious, unimportant or anti-social. We will be bound to the ends of the industrial system. The state will add its moral, and perhaps some of its legal, power to their enforcement. What will eventuate, on the whole, will be the benign servitude of the household retainer who is taught to love her mistress and see her interests as her own, and not the compelled servitude of the field hand. But it will not be freedom.

If, on the other hand, the industrial system is only a part, and relatively a diminishing part, of life, there is much less occasion for concern. Aesthetic goals will have pride of place; those who serve them will not be subject to the goals of the industrial system; the industrial system itself will be subordinate to the claims of these dimensions of life. Intellectual preparation will be for its own sake and not for the better service to the industrial system. Men will not be entrapped by the belief that apart from the goals of the industrial system – apart from the production of goods and income by progressively more advanced technical methods – there is nothing important in life.

John Kenneth Galbraith: *The New Industrial State*

7 Are Democratic Institutions Possible?

In the admitted absence of an adequate language of institutions, the hypothesis that institutions can be democratic may appear premature. In times like these, however, it may be necessary to take a chance. While all institutions tend to dominate, some do it less than others. Furthermore, other characteristics of institutions seem to be correlated with the degree to which these dominating tendencies are shown. The hypothesis of this chapter is that institutions can be identified in which the tendency toward domination can be restrained, and that encouragement of this kind of institution can foster the growth of a just and democratic society.

Institutions are so identified with hierarchy, control, privilege and exclusion that the very notion of democratic institutions seems strange.[1] Jeffersonian democracy was based on the relative absence of large institutions and came to grief with the growth of corporations and public bureaucracies. According to Galbraith and others, today's technology requires large institutions.[2] Must we choose, then, between institutional domination and a return to primitive means of production? There are some reasons to hope for escape from this dilemma. First, there have been at least quasi-democratic institutions: the Greek city state, the New England town, the Jeffersonian republic, some of the early temples, churches and religious fraternities, the Chinese market networks.[3] Second, there are some modern institutions which seem to serve democratic purposes: postal systems, telephone exchanges and road networks, for example. If Chinese markets and road networks do not appear to qualify for institutional status, this is at least partly because of the way we have been trained to think about institutions.

The history of institutions is a history of domination. Armies, temples, courts and empires established the institutional mould and, despite exceptions, their pattern has continued to determine man's thinking almost to the point of defining deviations from this pattern as non-institutional. Even people who admit that an organization which is neither hierarchical nor exclusive might be called an institution will argue that hierarchy and selective membership increase institutional efficiency. They probably do – for purposes of domination. Institutions which are better at dominating their members may also be better at dominating their rivals. Despite Pericles' eloquent claim for the superiority of Athenian democracy, Sparta won the war. The relatively democratic Greek city states were later conquered by much less democratic Rome. The record begins to get fuzzy with England's triumph over Spain and with the results of the two world wars. But even English history credits the better discipline of her navy, obtained partly by means of the lash, and the record is not yet closed on the battle between dictatorship and democracy. Currently the loudest clamour for control comes from the leadership of the democracies.

Hierarchy is, of course, related to size, both as cause and effect. Conquest and the subordination of one people to another was one of the earliest causes of hierarchy. Span of control is another factor. Size at least invites, if it does not require, more layers. If size is introduced as a correlate of hierarchy, the advantages of both in achieving domination are more apparent. But the admission that large hierarchically controlled institutions may be better at dominating others will not satisfy the adherents of hierarchy. They claim greater productive efficiency as well. This is a little like claiming that big sharks have more efficient digestive systems than little sharks because they succeed in eating them. Is General Motors more productive because it is bigger, or bigger because it is more productive? The answer is neither. It is bigger because it is the product of a merger; its size gives it the resources to dominate other companies that remain independent. It is not, in general, a more efficient producer, or it would not buy so many large and small components from smaller companies. Its size does help it to dominate the market, which in turn permits some economies of scale in production. General Motors is currently the most efficient player of the game in which it is engaged, just as the United States and Russia are currently the leaders in the world struggle for domination. No one would claim that both of these nations are models of efficiency in all other respects.

Basically, General Motors allows millions to play the game which only thousands could play when Veblen wrote his *The Theory of the Leisure Class*.[4] The thousands now play with Bentleys and Ferraris instead of Cadillacs and Chevrolets. If getting in on this game remains the major preoccupation of human beings, then General Motors must remain the model of institutional efficiency. But this is the same game, at the consumer level, as General Motors plays with other producers; the game of getting ahead of the Joneses. If men have other goals, then other institutional models are possible.

Consider American Telephone & Telegraph in contrast with General Motors. It is just as technical, just as profit oriented, just as large as General Motors, but there is a great difference in what the two companies do for and to their clients. The Telephone Company installs a phone and there it stays, whatever its age, shape or colour, unless the customer, for special reasons of his own, decides he wants a different model. The telephone subscriber pays a few dollars a month, and, unless he has teenage children, forgets about his phone until someone calls him or he wants to call someone else. The telephone doesn't have to be washed, waxed or serviced, except rarely, requires no insurance and is not liable to theft. It is not, on the other hand, a source of pride or envy, of concern or comfort, of thrill or trepidation. It is just there, in case it is needed to call next door or half way around the world, imposing no constraints on what is said and not intruding itself in any way into the use that is made of it. Anyone who has a dime or a friend or an honest face or an emergency can use it, even if he can't afford or doesn't want a phone of his own. And the essential service the user gets, the value it has for him, has nothing to do with what he pays or who he is. Clearly, people who are better off are more conveniently served, but the telephone network is essentially democratic – so long as it serves individuals rather than computers. The emergency user actually gets more value for his money than the regular subscriber.

How different the Cadillac or Chevrolet – not so much owned

as owning its possessor. Long before purchase, the which, with what, how much of this or that, dominate the family council. Subsequent payments dominate the family budget as much as the new acquisition controls family life. Triumphs and tragedies succeed each other in rapid succession as the new car succeeds or fails one relative test after another. Utility is usually the last concern. Car clubs are joined to avoid exposing the new member of the family to the dangers of the parking lot. Gasoline mileage is important only as a comparison point. Emission of lead and other air-borne poisons is not even considered.

Human nature? Perhaps. But elsewhere people compete on horses, or on foot, or with sticks or stones, without surrendering their lives (including employment, taxes, education, the condition of the air, water and land on which they live) to the producers of these horses, sticks or stones. And yet, human nature is involved. The automobile, like the modern house or household utility, is too big a toy to be resisted. Offered even in exchange for submission to its supplier, it is as hard to resist as were the early cults with their idols, incense and temple prostitutes. Life is hard and dull and what else is there to relieve the tedium?

This is one of three traditional ways of dominating men. The others are force and the withholding of necessities. Force is used between nations to obtain or maintain relative overall advantage. Withholding of necessities is used to assure ourselves of the menial services of the poor. The grown-up plaything game is used on us to keep us available for use against other countries and the lower class.

It is important to recognize the various aspects of the game. International competition, inter-class competition and interpersonal competition are all related. The first requires the military institution, the second the police and penal institutions, and the third requires General Motors. What these games or processes and institutions have in common is the advantage they try to establish for one group or individual over another. In the case of international and class conflict this is quite straightforward. The means by which individuals are placed in competition with each other are a little more complex.

Keeping up with, or surpassing, the Joneses is simple enough. There is a variation of this game, however, in which not the

Joneses but the whole human race becomes the reference group – when men try to play God. This might also be called the escape from reality game. It can be played with alcohol or drugs, with sex, with many kinds of variously staged fantasy and with grown-up playthings that fly, roar, tickle the imagination or titillate the senses. Keeping up with the Joneses may, in fact, be just a variant of this game, with the sense of superiority, or inferiority, coming from advantage over some rather than all.

What all forms of advantage have in common is that they exact a price for the advantage as well as for the product which provides it. When the advantage is permanent this price must be paid continuously. When the advantage is on all counts the price is total. The point is made elegantly in the Faust legend and the theme appears throughout human mythology. It provides the touchstone for distinguishing democratic from dominating institutions.

Democratic institutions offer a service, satisfy a need, without conferring advantage over others or conveying the sense of dependence that institutions such as welfare agencies do. They take the form of networks rather than production systems; networks which provide an opportunity to do something rather than make and sell a finished product. Public communication and transportation systems are examples, as are water works and sewers, electricity and gas distribution systems and general markets which facilitate the flow of various kinds of goods. Public utilities are democratic institutions if they are truly public and provide something really useful.

Everyone has access to a true public utility, either free of charge or at a fee everyone can afford. Access is at the option and initiative of the user, who may also leave the service when he wishes. Use is not obligatory. The most useful products such as electricity or water can be used for a variety of purposes. So can roads or the mails. Public utility networks show true economy of scale. The bigger they get and the more of the population they serve the more useful they are for everyone. Water and sewer systems which might seem to be exceptions are seen not to be when public health is considered. Superhighways, as opposed to road networks, are false public utilities. They are actually the private preserves of car owners, built partly at public expense.

Utilities serve basic, universal needs. Everyone needs water, power, communication, transport, food, raw materials, a place to exchange fabricated products and many other things. Nevertheless, basic needs are limited. They cannot be indefinitely multiplied. They can, therefore, be satisfied without exhausting all available time, labour, raw materials and human energy. After they have been satisfied there are things left for people to do, if and when they like, and there are remaining resources for doing them. The managers of democratic institutions can and must be largely responsive to the expressed desires of their clients.

Institutions which confer or maintain advantage over others fit a description almost diametrically opposed to that above. They tend to be production systems rather than networks. If networks are involved they have the secondary purpose of distributing a particular product. Access is limited and access costs are frequently high. Once on it isn't easy to get off; participation is often either obligatory or addictive.[5] The product tends to be specific, elaborate and all-purpose. There are important diseconomies of scale. At some point extension of the service to new clients becomes a disservice to former clients. The needs served are not basic but at least partly induced. Once induced, however, these needs are open-ended and can never be fully satisfied. Surfeit leads to excess rather than to satiation. Dominating institutions tend, therefore, to become total, to exhaust the life space of human beings and the life-sustaining capacity of the biosphere. The managers of dominating institutions must take and maintain the initiative. Clients must be seduced, manipulated or coerced. True initiative or choice on the part of clients tends to disrupt the maintenance requirements of dominating institutions.

Most actual institutions fit these opposing prototypes only partially. Some fit fairly well, including certain public utilities, on the one hand, and military establishments, prisons and asylums, on the other. Most products, services and institutions fall somewhere in between. Automobiles, modern houses and home utilities are not merely pawns in a status game, but are also useful. Making long-distance calls on credit cards, on the other hand, may be pure one-upmanship. The management of the telephone company and its institutional advertising differ little from those of General Motors, which also produces buses as well as private cars. The buses are, however, almost incidental. The policies of General Motors and its role in society are determined by the private automobile, considered not primarily as transportation – as Henry Ford viewed the Model T – but as status symbol. With the development of the video-phone, the telephone company could easily embark on the same route. A videophone is not for everyone, and might seem to require private viewing space. This in turn could lead to elaboration not unlike that which has afflicted the automobile. If the choice were left to management, there is little doubt that A T & T would follow the route of General Motors. The management of a true public utility must be at the service and command of its clientele. The management of a dominating institution must manage its clientele as well as its personnel. The choice is a fateful one. It is, hopefully, not too late for the public to choose.

The choice is not between high and low technology. It is not necessarily between private and public management, of either 'public' utilities or 'private' factories for necessary products. It is a choice of shopping lists, of the kinds and varieties of products that will be available. An unlimited market basket for the rich is not compatible with freedom for either the rich or poor. But this metaphor is inexact. The 'unlimited' market basket can be filled only with those products of high technology which enough people can be induced to buy. It can, of course, be filled with custom-made products for those who can afford them, but even these will be the products of an inherited artisanship, living on the past. A vigorous artisanship cannot survive in unrestricted competition with high technology. The choice ultimately is between two completely different styles of life. One is egalitarian, pluralistic and relatively sparse in the kinds of products and services it provides. People have to do things for themselves, but have time and freedom to do what they want. The other kind of life is based on a unified hierarchy of privilege, maintained by international, inter-class and inter-personal competition. The kinds of competition are limited and highly structured but the prizes are relatively glamorous, at least on the surface.

It may seem idealistic in the extreme to believe that people who have the second option already in their hands will voluntarily exchange it for the first. Yet there are signs that this could happen. But the choice may not be entirely voluntary. Pollution of the environment, pressure from the underprivileged and the horrors of war may help to decide the issue. However, blind forces cannot achieve intelligent solutions of issues. Only intelligence can do that. This is why education is so important, and why it cannot be left to schools.

Schools are themselves dominating institutions rather than opportunity networks. They develop a product which is then sold to their clients as education. Concentrating on children gives them a less critical clientele, to which they offer the prizes that other dominating institutions produce. Parents want these prizes for their children, even more than for themselves, and can be sold a rosy future even more easily than a current illusion. Seen at a distance the fallacies of competition are harder to perceive clearly. Foreigners can have what we have if they will follow the course we have followed. Workers can achieve our standard of living if they will educate themselves to earn it. Our children can have what we couldn't have if they will prepare themselves to produce it. These propositions sound so plausible and yet are so patently false when viewed in perspective. An open-ended consumption race must always result in a hound who gets the rabbit, a bunched pack in the middle who get some of the shreds, and a train of stragglers. This must be the outcome in terms of nations, of classes and of individuals. Schools not only cloud this perspective, they actively foster the illusions which contradict it. They prepare children precisely for interpersonal, inter-class and international competition. They produce adults who believe they have been educated and who, in any case, have no remaining resources with which to pursue their education.

Men had better be without education than be educated by their rulers; for this education is but the mere breaking in of the steer to the yoke; the mere discipline of the hunting dog, which by dint of severity is made to forego the strongest impulse of his nature, and instead of devouring his prey, to hasten with it to the feet of his master.

Thomas Hodgkins, 1823

8 Education for Freedom

Alternatives to schools must be more economical than schools: cheap enough so that everyone can share in them. They must also be more effective so that lower costs do not imply less education. Monopoly must be avoided. The school system must not be replaced by another dominant system: alternatives must be plural. There should be competition between alternatives, but some of them, at least, should not involve competition between students, especially for lifetime prizes. One student should not learn at the expense of another, nor should success for one student imply failure for another. Alternatives to schools should not manipulate individuals but, on the contrary, should prepare individuals to direct and re-create institutions, including their governments. Education should not be separated from work and the rest of life, but integrated with them. Educational environments should be protective only to an unavoidable degree. Education should not, primarily, prepare for something else nor be a by-product of something else. It should be a self-justified activity designed to help man gain and maintain control of himself, his society and his environment.

Alternatives to schools must, above all, allow everyone the opportunity to learn what he needs to know in order to act intelligently in his own interests. No educational programme can guarantee that everyone will learn what he needs to know, much less that if he did he would act upon it. It should be possible, however, to keep open the opportunity for such learning, not only during the youth but throughout the lifetime of every man. One of the major complications arises from the almost universal predilection to feel that we know better than others what is in their interests. Schools, for example, are almost wholly concerned with trying to teach some people what other people want them to know. Those who make the decisions about what should be taught in school pretend to know and to act in the interest of the learners. It should be clear by now that either they do not know or that, if they do, they act in contradiction to their knowledge.

What man's true interests are and what he needs to know to pursue them are the starting points not only of educational philosophy but also of any general philosophical basis for social policy. Defining freedom, in its clearest if not its most complete sense, as freedom *from* rather than freedom *for*, leads to a definition of basic values and factual propositions in largely negative terms. The question becomes, as Paul Goodman says, not what shall we do but what will we tolerate.[1] Philosophies which state in positive terms what is and what should be seem to lead to the constraint of one human being by another, to the imposition of enlightenment upon the heathen. A philosophy based on the right of maximum freedom from human constraint begins by denying the right of any man to impose either truth or virtue upon another.

The implications of such a philosophy of freedom are very far-reaching. They include, for example, denial of the right to monopolize anything which other men need, since such monopoly is and always has been used to violate their freedom. Needs, moreover, cannot be restrictively defined as those things immediately needed to sustain life. Denial of information, for example, leads to denial of fresh air, pure water and nutritious food. Information denial is being used in the modern world – generally, consistently and systematically – to keep people from knowing, and thereby from getting what they need, of even such elementary things as air, water and food.

A philosophy of freedom need not specify in advance which positive things must be done in order to avoid the constraint of one man by another. It can reserve the application of the test of freedom to specific situations.

The world of schools conceives the problem of education as one of inducing students to learn what they are supposed to know. From this point of view, it seems nonsensical to think of people as being blocked from knowing and learning. Yet clearly they are. Most of the people of the world sweat their lives out on land which belongs to others, constantly in debt to their landlords, with no control over the prices of what they buy or sell, helpless in their misery and kept helpless not only by denial of information and opportunity to learn but by deliberate distortion of the facts of their lives. Witch doctors, priests, politicians and purveyors of profitable nostrums vie with each other to keep these people sunk in their ignorance and unaware of their true condition. They are aided in these attempts by the physical misery in which their victims are forced to live, misery so great and so hopeless that it must somehow be justified, somehow disguised, in order to make it bearable.

Education for these people does not consist primarily in learning to read, but in learning to understand and to do something about their miserable situation. This may involve learning to read but it must obviously include other things, without which the ability to read would not be of any real value. Suppose that a few children in such an environment do learn to read and thus escape. This does nothing to help those who stay behind to breed more children.

Much of what people in this situation need to know, in order to basically improve their lot, is actively withheld or hidden from them, even though the resources for learning to read may be offered. Paulo Freire found in working with Brazilian peasants that they immediately learned to read those words which helped them to discover their true life situation.[2] Unearthing this vocabulary requires an insight into the lives of these peasants which penetrates the secrets, misinformation and mystification with which their landlords, priests and political leaders surround them. Paulo Freire's clients no sooner learned to read than they organized peasant leagues through which they tried to bargain with their employers. Although they were scrupulously careful to observe the law and the customs of the region, their employers, government authorities and the Church turned upon them in unison. Their leaders were fired and jailed, while the Church denied its sacraments to members of the league until Protestant missionaries began to make converts among them.

This sounds like an exaggerated case, but Paulo Freire's Brazilian clients are representative, in their essential features, of over half the people of the earth. Freire himself had to flee Brazil when the present military government took over. Although invited to Chile by the governing Christian Democratic Party of that country, he was not allowed to work freely. After a year at Harvard he is now with the World Council of Churches in Geneva, safely and unhappily insulated from the poor and uneducated masses of the world.

This is easy to understand, given the structure of society and the probable consequences of educating its improverished majority. Withholding education from these masses may still appear to be a special case, justified by the inability of society to cope with the impact of education on such a massive scale. But this is not a special case. We treat our own children in the same way and we ourselves are so treated by our governments, public bureaucracies and privately owned corporations.

We take as great pains to hide the facts of life from our children as do the Brazilian landlords to hide them from their peasants. Like them, we not only hide and distort facts but invoke the assistance of great institutions and elaborate mythologies. Facts of life are not confined to sex: about this we are becoming less inhibited even with children. But relative incomes of families on the block, the neighbourhood power structure, why father didn't get his promotion or mother her chairmanship, why Jimmy is smoking pot or Susie is having an out of town vacation: these things which children perversely want to know are obviously not for them. Neither is ballet at the expense of reading, karate in place of maths, or the anatomy of flies as a substitute for botany out of a book. Schools are obviously as much designed to keep children from learning what really intrigues them as to teach them what they ought to know. As a result, children learn to read and do not read, learn their numbers and hate mathematics, shut themselves off in classrooms and do their learning in cloakrooms, hangouts and on the road. The exceptions are those who are allowed to learn to read when and what they wish, and to do likewise with mathematics, science, music, etc.

We ourselves are treated no better than our children. Attempts to get the contents of cans and boxes clearly labelled are treated as attacks on private enterprise. Any real probing of foreign policy is labelled subversive, while the basic facts are hidden behind the screen of national security. The enemies of every military power in the world know more about its military capacities and intentions than is available to the makers of its own laws. Spies, bellhops, charwomen, valets and ladies' maids are the privileged exceptions to the conspiracy of secrecy in which we live.

There are, of course, the best of reasons for all the secrecy and mystification. Children might be permanently scarred by premature exposure to death, suffering, sex or the sordid facts of economic and political life. Mechanics might be embarrassed if car owners were given detailed descriptions of their own motor cars. A little knowledge is dangerous, not only for laymen, but for their doctors, lawyers and accountants as well. If customers were allowed to know what they were buying, then competitors could also find it out. If national security barriers were lowered, the enemy would learn even more at lower cost. These reasons range from valid to ludicrous but even the valid ones are valid only in the context of the society in which we live. In this society, Paulo Freire is a threat and so is the free education of our children and of ourselves. At present, this education is not free. People are systematically prevented from learning those things which are most important for them to know. They are deliberately misled by elaborate distortions of facts and by the propagation of religious, political and economic mythologies which make it extraordinarily difficult to get a clear glimpse of relevant truth. Protestants see clearly through the Catholic smoke screen. Capitalists have no difficulty in seeing how the communists brainwash their victims. Englishmen and Frenchmen see through each other's Common Market machinations without the slightest trouble. Only our own camouflage confuses us.

It might be said in rebuttal that every society must have its secrets, its mythologies, its propaganda. Some information will always be off limits for children and for adults. We have a choice of what will be hidden and obscured, but not of whether anything will be. This may be true, but it is not true by definition. Only where there are major differences of interest and where one group has the power to distort reality does it seem inevitable that this will occur. All societies in recorded history have been of this kind. All have had ruling classes which exploited other members of their own populations and fought with other élites for the privilege of exploitation. Societies need not be organized in this way. In fact most current societies claim that they are not. The ideal of a non-exploiting, mutual-interest society has long been proclaimed and many people believe that such a society is possible. If it is, then there should be no need for major systems of secrecy nor for mythologies whose major purpose is to distort the truth. In such a society, education for freedom should be possible. It may also be that such a society can be created only by men who have been educated for freedom, by whatever means. This possibility and hope justifies the proclamation of the ideal of education for freedom, even in a society in which it does not truly fit. The hope stems from the fact that our society *does* proclaim the ideals of justice and freedom. In the name of these ideals it is possible to call for free education, realizing that it can be fully achieved only as greater social justice is also achieved, and that each can and must be instrumental in the achievement of the other.

Specific barriers to information are not as important as mythologies and the institutions through which these are propagated. In the case of tribal societies, these mythologies take the form of what we generally and somewhat inaccurately label witchcraft. Various systems of witchcraft contain much valid knowledge and significant powers to cure the sick, solve social problems and give meaning to the lives of people. They also, however, serve to hide the power structures of their respective societies, disguise the dominant means of exploitation, and make people feel that the evils they suffer are inevitable and, sometimes, even for their own good.

The major traditional religions, with all of their differences from witchcraft and from each other, serve the same social purposes both positive and negative. Catholicism as it affects the peasant populations of Latin America illustrates the point very aptly because, in many regions, it is Catholicism in name only. Actually it is often merely an overlay of popular saint culture upon a base of indigenous witchcraft, the content of the Catholic and witchcraft elements of the amalgams varying from one region to another.[3] The social functions performed by these amalgams are the same, however, with no discernible differences in efficacy. They all effect cures, control anti-social impulses, or re-establish order when the controls fail, and provide a structure of meaning for celebration of birth, death, marriage and other critical events in the lives of individuals. Most important of all, from a social point of view, they legitimize ownership of the land by the rich, condone and justify the privileges enjoyed by the élites at the expense of the poor, exalt the charitable acts of the élite and their symbolic roles in religious, political, economic and familial affairs. They provide the peasants with a set of after-life rewards to console them for their misery in the present life, represent their current suffering as the will of God and acquiescence in these sufferings as the height of virtue.

There are, of course, many Catholic priests in Latin America whose behaviour contradicts every line of the above description, who castigate the rich and assist, arouse and lead the peasants in their search for justice. These priests are sometimes killed, more often locked up as mad, and still more often assigned to innocuous duties or dismissed. Occasionally their work is welcomed and supported by bishops who agree with them.

When Latin American peasants move to the cities and become urban workers they are converted in large numbers to a variety of fundamentalist Protestant sects. Even Catholic employers frequently prefer these converts as workers and hire them selectively. They are likely to be more sober, faithful to their wives and families, earnest about their work, about keeping their children in school, acquiring possessions and getting ahead in the world. Their behaviour supports perfectly Weber's hypothesis on the relationship between Protestantism and industrialization. The personally permissive nominal Catholicism – so perfectly adjusted to rural Latin America and so sharply in contrast with its counterparts in rural Ireland and northern Spain – is poorly suited to Sao Paulo, Buenos Aires, Mexico City and the lesser industrial centres of Latin America. So is the more sophisticated urban Catholicism of Latin American cities with its emphasis on the rights of labour, the obligations of the employer and, in general, on social justice in the modern industrial world. The teachings of some of the older Protestant sects are no more in the interests of urban employees and these sects make fewer converts among the workers.

It may seem odd that workers join the sects whose teachings are in their employers' interest rather than their own. This is, first of all, because employers select as workers the members of these sects. It is, secondly, because relatively powerless workers psychologically need a religion which will reconcile the contradictions between their employers' interests and their own.

In Europe, the United States, Japan and the former British dominions, religion no longer plays the major role in adjusting men to their societies. This role falls to mythologies of science, professionalism, consumption, the state, the corporation, the welfare agency and, above all, the school. The mass media and the advertising industry are, of course, important but they are the carriers and arrangers of the various myths and do not provide their substance.

Progress toward freedom occurs in cycles. At some point in the cycle, part of the myth is discredited. Peasants move to the city, a scandal occurs, some defector lifts the veil, a penetrating analysis is made. People glimpse the truth, make demands, win concessions, are a little better off and not so much in need of hiding reality from themselves. The stage is set for a new lifting of the veil and a new cycle. Men do not arrive suddenly at total truth nor at total justice. Myth is replaced by myth, institution by institution, injustice by injustice, but when things go well, each myth is less embracing, each institution more transient, each injustice more bearable and less in need of being mythologized.

This does not mean that change must come gradually or slowly. When major myths and institutions are replaced change may be swift and radical – radical enough to be called revolution, regardless of the degree of violence involved. Violence is not the proper mark of revolution, nor are dramatic changes in the political façade. Too often these occur accompanied by no significant changes at all in myths or institutions, or in relationships between oppressors and oppressed. Significant change occurs when people stop believing in what may once have been true, but has now become false; when they withdraw support from institutions which may once have served them but no longer do; when they refuse to submit to what may once have been fair terms but which are no longer. Such changes, when they occur, are a product of true education. The problem is not one of motivating people to learn what others want them to learn. It is rather to provide the resources which enable them to learn what they want and need to know.

At the treaty of Lancaster, in Pennsylvania, anno 1744, between the Government of Virginia and the Six Nations, the commissioners from Virginia acquainted the Indians by a speech, that there was at Williamsburg a college with a fund for educating Indian youth; and that if the chiefs of the Six Nations would send down half a dozen of their sons to that college, the government would take care that they be well provided for, and instructed in all the learning of the white people.

The Indians' spokesman replied:
'We know that you highly esteem the kind of learning taught in those colleges, and that the maintenance of our young men, while with you, would be very expensive to you. We are convinced, therefore, that you mean to do us good by your proposal and we thank you heartily.

'But you, who are wise, must know that different nations have different conceptions of things; and you will not therefore take it amiss, if our ideas of this kind of education happen not to be the same with yours. We have had some experience of it; several of our young people were formerly brought up at the colleges of the northern provinces; they were instructed in all your sciences; but, when they came back to us, they were bad runners, ignorant of every means of living in the woods, unable to bear either cold or hunger, knew neither how to build a cabin, take a deer, nor kill an enemy, spoke our language imperfectly, were therefore neither fit for hunters, warriors, nor counsellors; they were totally good for nothing.
'We are however not the less obligated by your kind offer, though we decline accepting it, and to show our grateful sense of it, if the gentlemen of Virginia will send us a dozen of their sons, we will take care of their education, instruct them in all we know, and make men of them.'

Benjamin Franklin: *Remarks concerning the Savages of North America*

9 What People Need to Know

The title of this chapter has a double meaning. It refers both to the objectives of education and to the resources required to pursue these objectives. They are discussed together because, as will be seen, they are intimately interrelated and cannot properly be separated. Education should lead to a world based on freedom and justice; where freedom means a minimum of constraint by others, and justice means a distribution of wealth, power and other values consistent with this kind of freedom.

Men in society necessarily constrain each other. The problem is one of defining the boundary between one man's fist and the other's nose. Where fists and noses are literally in question, this is easy, and it is not much harder in other matters, so long as men are assumed to be enough alike to validate the golden rule. If we assume that all men value health, wealth, skill, power, respect and affection, then justice requires that no man should have so much of any of these as to deprive another of his share. This does not mean that all shares must be equal. Monogamy would not have to be restrictively defined. The test could be whether anyone is deprived of a mate by the existence of a Mormon or Tibetan household. There can also be other trade-offs. A true urbanite might be glad to trade his share of acreage for a Manhattan apartment. Obviously, no one else – his children for example – should be bound by such a trade.

The details of a just, free world must be based upon the freely given and mutual consent of relative equals, of persons who, as far as possible, have equal knowledge and equal understanding of what their consent implies. Educational objectives must be defined, not only in terms of how to maintain such a world, but in terms of how to attain it and keep it growing. Education must be a major instrument in the development of a just world. The basic objective of education must be an understanding of the world we live in and the world we hope for, understanding which can lead to effective action. Such action is assumed to be voluntary and cooperative, but unavoidable conflict is not ruled out. The education in question must prepare individuals to act with others as well as by themselves. But before a man can engage in intelligent collective action he must understand his own situation, not as a social atom, but as member of a family and other groups.

People understand the world by means of language. Not exclusively but in the main, especially if language is broadly defined, as Suzanne Langer defines it, to include music, dancing, poetry and other affective modes of communication.[1] But language is used, as we have seen, to obscure and to distort reality as well as to render it lucid. People must have the opportunity to learn to use language critically – in such a way as to reflect upon the thing discussed and also upon the language in which it is discussed. It is not so important how much or how many languages are learned as it is to learn not to be naïve. At the same time, it is not enough to be shrewd about only a few things, as the peasant or the beggar often is. A minimum breadth of language skill is necessary in order to protect one's interest in the world; to understand one's situation well enough to act upon it significantly. This is impossible without some knowledge of physical science, politics, economics and psychology.

As these disciplines are talked about today it would, obviously, be impossible for everyone to learn their languages. But this is because these languages have become so esoteric that those who go to the trouble of learning them can then use them to confuse and exploit others. Almost everyone knows what aspirin is except when doctors prescribe it as acetylsalicylic acid. Everyone knows what damage is except when lawyers call it a tort. Many specialists, of course, are free of any intention to confuse or exploit. Furthermore, specialized languages are clearly necessary for the creation of new knowledge. Specialists cannot forget, however, that they practise their specialty at the sufferance of the rest of society and that if they fail to maintain effective communication, they open society to exploitation – directly or indirectly – by practitioners of their specialty. New knowledge may benefit or injure mankind depending on how it is used. The creators of new knowledge are as obliged, therefore, to create a language in which new knowledge can be generally communicated as to create one in which new knowledge can be developed. A famous scientist said recently that any scientific concept can be explained to anyone by someone who himself understands it concretely. This does not mean, however, the kind of simplifying textbook explanations that characterize today's schools. The outlines of the great classics, best-sellers in every university bookstore, illustrate the point. If books written to divert voluntary readers had never been made classics, from which curricula were then constructed, there would be no need for outlines. The peasants of old Russia would have understood and preferred Dostoyevsky in the original.

But the problem cannot be fully understood at this level. It is necessary to go back to the peasant culture in which Paulo Freire worked, and even beyond this to the origins of this culture. Freire calls the rural culture of Latin America a Culture of Silence. By this he means that the rural masses, having been deprived of any real voice in the matters which concern them most, have forgotten how to speak or even to think about these matters except in terms of the rationalizing mythologies supplied by their superiors. In Freire's terms they have lost the 'word'. The term is used here as it is in the first verse of the Gospel according to St John: 'In the beginning was the word and the word was with God and the word was God.' To understand how the word might be lost to a whole class of men, it is necessary only to remember the origins of this class in the twin institutions of slavery and serfdom. Slaves and serfs were allowed to sing, to chant, to chatter and to gossip – and in ancient times much more – but they were not allowed to say anything serious about their own condition or about the society which kept them in this condition. For generations the children of this class were raised without reference to such matters, and even with conscious repression by parents of references that innocent children might make. It is easy to see how the word was lost to slaves and serfs and their successors.

The essentials of the Culture of Silence are reflected in the Culture of Childhood. Children, too, are allowed to sing and chatter, but not to know or talk about grown-up things. Theirs too is a culture of silence but, at the higher social levels, more like that of the Greek slaves in Roman times who were allowed to learn everything except the arts of war and politics and who might even, after years of proof of loyalty, be freed.

Similarities between children, slaves and peasants have often been noted and have served even as the basis for ethnic myths, explaining the supposed inferiority of lower classes and oppressed races in terms of their childlike character, thus justifying the maintenance of domination over them. The mythic character of such beliefs is completely exposed by anthropologists, such as Lévi-Strauss, who show that the intellectual systems and accomplishments of so-called primitives are as complex as those of scientifically and technically advanced populations.[2] The kinship, plant and animal classification systems which are learned in these cultures are as difficult to learn as any of our scientific and technical codes. For us they would be much harder.

People learn what they need and are allowed to learn. What they need is a function of the culture they live in and of their role within it. What they are allowed to learn is also a function of this culture. But cultures contain ideals, and these as well as the institutions which pervert them help to determine what needs to be and may be learned.

In a free, just world, or in progress toward one, all people need to know how the universal values of their society are created and distributed and how the methods of creation and distribution are governed, i.e. how the society is governed. Laswell and Kaplan in their book *Power and Society* list such universal values as well-being, wealth, power and respect, and give examples of the processes by which each value is converted into others. Power, for example, may be based upon respect or obtained through bribery. Wealth may be obtained through productivity or extorted from others by threats to their well-being.[3] Not everyone needs to know all of the techniques of how each value is created and exchanged but they do need to know enough to prevent any group of specialists from attaining a dominant role – or to reduce this role if it has already been attained. Basic educational policy needs to be concerned with providing universal access to only this much learning, and with preventing obstacles to any more specialized learning which individuals might choose. To put this more concretely: basic educational policy must guarantee not only freedom of access but an adequate supply of the resources required for everyone to learn how society really works. Provision of resources for more specialized learning can be left to specialized groups and agencies of the society, as long as access to these resources is not restricted.

The universal educational objectives stated above imply both much more and much less learning than occurs today, either in schools or in the normal process of growing up outside them. Very few people today learn anything about international finance, practical politics or military strategy, or about who marries whom for what reasons. Few people learn much about the foods and poisons they eat, drink or breathe, about why they feel as they do or why other people treat them as they do.

At the same time, people all over the world are learning the details of elaborate kinship networks, plant classification systems, agricultural folklore, histories and geographies, categories of arts no longer practised, age-old myths and superstitions and a host of other things. Some of these things may need to continue to be learned, but only by particular individuals or groups. How society works needs to be learned by every responsible member of a free, just world. As the world changes, the necessary content of universal education will also change. The present formulation is merely illustrative, but will serve to indicate the kinds of information which must be disclosed and the kinds of learning resources which must be provided.

The secular significance of the great religious teachers of the past can be seen in the important role of disclosure in true education. Apart from the transcendental content of their teaching, Moses, Jesus, Mohammed, Gautama, Lao Tse, to mention only a few of the most famous, were able to disclose the significant truths of their time to millions of people. Each of their teachings was, of course, subsequently used to obscure the very enlightenment they brought, to justify what they denounced, and to convict those whom they justified. Nevertheless, the truths they revealed could never again be totally hidden. Today's injustice stands convicted by their teachings and today's ideals are built upon them. Their teachings were not esoteric. Many of their contemporaries must have seen what they saw, felt what they felt, but lacked the security to trust their judgement, the courage to speak their mind, or the charisma to attract disciples.

In our time, the great teachers have spoken in secular terms. Marx, Freud, Darwin, to again name only the most famous, have revealed to millions truths that many others sensed but could not equally well express. Thanks in part to the great teachers of the past, today's significant truths lie closer to the surface. They are there for everyone to see. The veneer which covers them is frequently transparent; the hypocrisy with which they are disguised is often so blatant as to be insulting. Today, no genius is required to discover, reveal and proclaim the truths which could set men free. But it still takes doing. This is the role of the true teacher, the one educational resource which will always be in short supply.

Aside from people who discover truth, all educational resources are potentially plentiful. Schools make them scarce and costly, but freed from the perverse packaging which schools impose, there are enough resources to provide lifetime education for everyone.

Schooling has become the most costly of human enterprises. More people are enrolled in school than are employed in agriculture. More man-hours are spent in the classroom than in the fields. If the time of students is valued at its market potential, more money is tied up in schooling than in agriculture, industry or warfare. Schools are so costly because they separate what should be combined and combine what should be kept separate. Schools separate learning from work and play, parcel the world into subject matters and divide learners into teachers and students. They then package subject matters into curricula; package baby-sitting, skill modelling, administration, pedagogy, research and intellectual leadership into teaching; and package fraternities, athletics, professional training and intellectual life into colleges and universities.

Separation of learning from other activities is the most serious error. Learning occurs naturally at work and at play, but must be artificially stimulated when separated from them. Learning occurs naturally in the course of encountering real-world problems, but when these are subdivided into mathematics, economics, accounting and business practice they become so artificial that for most people learning can be induced only at great cost. Learning occurs naturally in the course of true teaching, but only with great difficulty in the role of classroom student or classroom teacher.[4]

Every thing and every person in the world is a learning resource. All are needed but all are plentiful, in relation to the need for them, unless deliberately made scarce. Educationally, things are of two kinds: ordinary things to which only occasional access must be provided and special things to which regular access is required. The special things may be records such as books, tapes, discs, films, papers, punch cards, computer memories. Other types of special things are instruments for producing or interpreting records such as pencils, typewriters, presses, tape recorders or computers; toys and equipment for games; natural elementary things such as rocks, sand and water. People can also be classified as ordinary or special educational resources but here the need for access is just the opposite as in the case of things. Ordinary people are commonly needed and require regular access while only occasional access is required to the special people. These special people are the ones we call educators, who have a very different role in the organization of educational resources we shall propose than they now have in the service of schools.

For the purpose of organizing access, educational resources are conveniently grouped into special and general things, and into three types of people: skill models, peers and educators. These classes of resources involve either different problems of access or else need to be kept distinct in order to avoid the packaging and artificial shortages which now make schooling so expensive.

An Expedient was therefore offered, that since Words are only Names for *Things*, it would be more convenient for all Men to carry about them, such *Things* as were necessary to express the particular Business they are to discourse on. And this Invention would certainly have taken Place, to the great Ease as well as Health of the Subject, if the Women in Conjunction with the Vulgar and Illiterate had not threatened to raise a Rebellion, unless they might be allowed the Liberty to speak with their Tongues, after the Manner of their Forefathers: Such constant irreconcilable Enemies to Science are the common People.

However, many of the most Learned and Wise adhere to the new Scheme of expressing themselves by *Things*; which hath only this Inconvenience attending it; that if a Man's Business be very great, and of various Kinds, he must be obliged in Proportion to carry a greater Bundle of *Things* upon his Back, unless he can afford one or two strong Servants to attend him. I have often beheld two of those Sages almost sinking under the Weight of their Packs, like Pedlars among us; who when they met in the Streets would lay down their Loads, open their Sacks, and hold Conversation for an Hour together; then put up their Implements, help each other to resume their Burthens, and take their Leave.

Jonathan Swift: *Gulliver's Travels*

10 Networks of Things

The prior division of things into those which have general and those which have special educational significance can be carried further. Those which have special educational value are again of two kinds: those which are symbol systems of some kind, and those which produce, translate, transmit or receive messages. These are things which serve as means of communicating not merely a specific message but large classes of messages. All objects can serve as means of communication but, as Swift pointed out in his 'Voyage to Laputa', some serve it better than others. Among those which serve it best are records, objects especially convenient for the storage of symbols. Records are so relatively easy and cheap to store and keep that they can be organized for quick access enormously more efficiently than the things they represent. This is the virtue of human brains, but also of computers, libraries, microfilm stores and the like. Large collections of records, such as central libraries or national archives, are like collective memories serving societies as brains serve individuals. Further organization of such record collections, by means of computers, is certain to increase their utility greatly and to warrant the comparison with human brains. Effective access to records is sure to become even more necessary to the educated man than it is today. Even today, records are very significant extensions of educated brains. Much that could be kept in human memory is deliberately passed on to these supplementary memory systems.

One of the things which makes almost unlimited universal education so potentially cheap is the great economy with which record systems of many types can now be organized for very rapid access, by almost unlimited numbers of people. Anyone who learns to use these systems, for which only elementary skills are needed – at least for certain levels of use – is then capable of carrying on his own education to almost any degree. This has always been true for people who knew how to read and to find books. The new development will simply make it easier. It may be worth noting that this too has always been true for anyone who knew how to observe and to find information. Reading merely made things easier, just as computers now do. They make things so much easier, however, that education can now become universal.

The quality of this education will depend only upon the quality and completeness of the records which are available to the public. Information upon which corporate and national advantage presumably depends will not be available. Neither will other information deemed vital by some groups for the maintenance of their advantage over others. These are problems which organization alone cannot solve.

Libraries are partial models for the organization of records and similar objects. Only an extension of the library system is necessary to enable these kinds of educational objects to be located and placed at the disposal of learners. But the scope of the extension required is very great. Libraries do not yet take full advantage of the ease and economy with which most records can now be reproduced. They are, of course, seriously handicapped by property rights and consequent restrictions on reproduction. These restrictions and the novelty of cheap reproduction methods account for the carry-over of the custodial tradition, which opens libraries to the charge of being more concerned with their records than with their clients. This tradition will have to be overcome, as will the tradition of serving an élite rather than the general public. The reading public is an élite and, because libraries were founded on books, an élite as well as a custodial tradition has limited their educational scope. It might not even be a good idea to use the name library in the network of special educational objects which must become one of the major institutional alternatives to schools.

In addition to vastly expanded directories and repositories of all kinds of records, we need similar means of access to other kinds of educational objects which have special value in the transmission of information. First among these are the instruments which play records, produce them or transmit their message. Books and papers are among the few records which do not require special decoders, although even with books, microfilm viewers are beginning to play a significant role. In the production of books and papers, however, instruments are indispensable. Pencils at least, much better typewriters, mimeograph machines or presses are necessary to produce written records. Universal access to these instruments is just as important as the ability to read what has been written. This is why freedom of the press was included in the American Bill of Rights. Its original purpose was to protect the rights of common people like Thomas Paine to make his ideas public; only later was it converted into protection of the freedom of the commercial press.

Most records other than books require instruments for their production and also for their use. Musical instruments and microphones may be needed to produce and record sound and record players to hear it. Typewriters and computers are needed for the production and reading of punch cards, tapes, disc-packs and other types of computer records. Cameras and projectors are another pair of basic instruments which can be combined with telescopes, microscopes, stethoscopes and many other devices, and can use television or telephone lines as transmitting devices. Then there are simpler kinds of materials for producing records such as paint and brushes, knives and chisels, knitting needles and string, a great variety of common tools and materials of the various practical and fine arts. Libraries have begun to stock some of these instruments and materials but usually only for privileged clients. They are much more commonly available for decoding than for the production of records and much more fully developed in the traditional media, related to books and written records, than in the newer communications techniques or in the huge variety of means of communication represented in the practical arts.

Message coding and decoding devices shade off into general types of instruments or machines which transform one kind of energy into another. Musical instruments and printing presses, for example, are not so strictly communications devices as tape recorders or typewriters. All general types of energy transformers have special educational value, not only because of their general usefulness in facilitating communication but also because they reveal some important features of the world; clocks, for example, reveal the relationship between motion and time, motors between motion and electricity, telescopes between distance and size. Names for relationships of this kind – but not confined to the world of physical science – make up the basic vocabulary of educated men.

Tools, instruments and machines are much less available now to most of the people of technological societies than they used to be. Specialized large-scale production removes them from the common scene. There are still artisans and mechanics in South America, Asia and Africa, but in Europe and North America they are disappearing rapidly. Not only children but also neighbours, friends, clients and passers-by are deprived of access to first-hand demonstrations, opportunities to experiment with tools and to see the insides of the gadgets which now come out of factories encased in shiny shells. Worse than this, many modern devices can no longer be taken apart without destroying them. They are not made to be repaired but to be replaced. As a result, modern man is becoming richer in devices and poorer in his understanding of them.[1] The multiplication of product shells and factory walls, behind which tools, instruments and machines are hidden, has the same effect, educationally, as the hiding of records behind the veils of national security and corporate privilege. The result is to deny people the information they need to act intelligently in their own interests. The reasons behind all this secrecy are also the same, even though the conscious motives may be different. Manufacturers guard their equipment and their products from the eyes of their customers, perhaps not consciously to keep them ignorant, but certainly in order to maintain an advantage in which ignorance is a critical factor.

Secrecy is by no means confined to capitalist countries. Professionals, managers and specialized workers guard their privileges as jealously as owners. The techniques of modern production play into their hands equally well and are, indeed, partly responsible quite apart from any conscious motivation. Large-scale production has, in and of itself, profoundly anti-educational implications, as Jane Jacobs points out in her *The Economy of Cities*.[2]

So long as large-scale production continues to monopolize tools, instruments, machines and other products which have special educational value, it will be necessary to include such products in educational directories and to arrange for general access to them. Vocational schools are one attempt to supply this access but they are far more expensive and much less educational than junkyards. Vocational schools can never serve the needs of the entire population while junkyards could, although today junkyards are in some respects more difficult of access.

Toys and games are a special class of objects with great potential for offsetting the educational disadvantages of a technological society. They can simulate many real objects and situations, sometimes to advantage and sometimes not. Traffic rules in the classroom, for example, may be a dangerously safe simulation of a truly dangerous situation. But simple toys and games, made easily and widely accessible at the option of individuals, could provide skill practice and intellectual insights with an effectiveness and economy not easy to match. Games have three great educational assets. First, they are a pleasant way of learning many skills, the practice of which might otherwise be onerous. Second, they provide a means of organizing activities among peers which make minimum demands upon leadership or authority. Finally, they are paradigms of intellectual systems, based on elements, operations and rules just as mathematical systems and other intellectual models are. People familiar with games can easily be introduced to a basic understanding of the most important models of science and mathematics. Games are, of course, open to the objection of stressing scientific and technological outlooks over those of nature and the humanities. Games are also open to the objection of pitting persons against each other and of producing losers and winners. It is doubtful, however, whether competition can or should be organized out of life. Games can be so organized as to equalize advantages and, thus, the pleasures of winning. While everyone still knows who is best, it is usually rather difficult for one person to be best at everything.

The problems of organizing access to toys and games fall largely into the ambit of libraries. Physical sports constitute an important exception, with problems similar to those involved where access to nature and natural things are involved.

Nature is not only becoming more distant, it is also being increasingly denatured, by exploitation and pollution on the one hand, and by attempts to sterilize adventure on the other. The exploitation and pollution of the natural environment have been well publicized and in terms of man's continued enjoyment of nature are of great importance. Educationally, however, cleaning up the environment may be worse than getting it dirty. The clean-up occurs at two levels. Protecting children from dirt, animals, birth, sickness, death and other natural things distorts their sense of what is real and natural. For the typical city child, nature is man-made like everything else. Even as an adult, he has decreasing opportunities to discover the truth. Jet planes and highways keep nature at a distance and even after he gets there, modern man's dude-ranch and stage-managed safari will do little to penetrate his urban aplomb. Only a few rivers, forests and mountain ranges remain unspoiled and these are being invaded. Nature can no longer be left to herself but has to be protected by man against man. Educational access complicates the problem of conservation, but education should be the main function of nature in the life of man. If proper boundaries are established between man and nature, and if his weapons are removed before he enters her, nature can continue to be man's mentor. For many people, a new guide will have to be written and new kinds of encounters devised. It is surprising and hopeful, however, to see what small enclaves of nature, truly protected, turn out to be viable.

Access to records, tools, machines, games, natural preserves and other extraordinarily useful educational objects is relatively easy to organize. Logical classifications already exist. Directories can easily be developed; storage in libraries and arrangements for other kinds of access can be made without major difficulty. But this leaves the whole of the rest of the world, not as concentratedly educational perhaps, but outweighing in its total educational value all of the special kinds of objects put together. This world of ordinary objects is one of the worlds men's minds must penetrate in order to act intelligently. The barriers to this world of ordinary objects are of several kinds. One is characterized by the automobile. Cities and many rural areas have become so unsafe for pedestrians, especially for children, that streets and roads – the physical paths to the world – are off limits to many of the world's inhabitants. If streets could again be opened to pedestrians, the city itself could again become a network of educational objects, the natural school which it has been throughout history. A second barrier, however, would still lie between the customers' area of the various shops and the workrooms where most of the really educational objects and processes are shut away. In older cities these barriers do not exist. The tradesman works where he sells, open to public view. In the modern city, however, there is yet a third line of defence. Many machines and processes are not there at all but hidden outside of the city or in places where only the persons who already know can find them. Directories which will locate this world for people who want to learn about it are indispensable, but even directories may not be easy to prepare and access will be still more difficult to arrange. For these most interesting objects are also the most carefully guarded – the scientific, military, economic or political objects hidden in laboratories, banks and governmental archives.

Secrets seem natural and inevitable in the world to which we are accustomed, but the cost of keeping them is very great. Science, for example, used to be a network of people, working all over the world, and exchanging information freely. One of the original premises of science, which has never been repealed, was that progress depends precisely upon the open sharing of the results of scientific work. Now the members as well as the artifacts of the scientific community have been locked into national and corporate prisons, impoverishing even the citizens of these nations and the stockholders of these corporations. The special privileges they gain are more than offset by the barriers to the growth of knowledge. In a world controlled and owned by nations and corporations, only limited access to educational objects will ever be possible. Increased access to those objects which can be shared, however, may increase men's insight enough to enable them to break through these ultimate educational barriers.

Learning is but an adjunct to ourself,
And where we are our learning likewise is.

William Shakespeare

11 Networks of People

Although people could learn a lot in a world where things were freely accessible to them, it would still be helpful to have the assistance of other people. Each person might eventually learn to type, given a typewriter, but each might learn to type in a different way. Having a typist who could demonstrate the skill would help to avoid this, especially if more than one learner took advantage of the same model. If that happened, those two could compare notes and, thus, learn something from each other. If, finally, there were in addition to the skill model and the two learners, someone who had taught typing before, had compared the progress of various learners, and drawn some valid conclusions, this person might also be useful in reducing the time required to learn to type.

The indispensable resource for learning to type is, of course, the typewriter itself. The skill model, while not indispensable, might, nevertheless, reduce the learning time by quite a bit and improve the final product as well. The fellow learner, the peer, is also important, especially in providing motivation to learn and the opportunity for practice. Less important than the others is the typing teacher.

Schools reverse this kind of logic. They do not, it is true, try to teach typing without a typewriter, but they frequently try to teach foreign languages without the help of anyone who can speak them, without anyone to speak to in them, and without anything to say in them that could not just as well be said in the native language of the learner. Geography is similarly taught without benefit of people who come from the places in question. Music is taught without instruments or musicians, science and mathematics by people who do not know them. Schools assume that the indispensable resource for learning is the teacher. Ideally this teacher should have the essential equipment for the practice of the skill and should also be able to demonstrate the skill, but these are secondary considerations. The need for learning peers is given lip service but little use is made of peers in the learning process.

Schools are not just wilfully perverse. Learning a skill, learning to practise it with someone else who is learning it, and learning how others have learned it are three different things, sometimes related but also frequently not. Schools try to find teachers who combine all three kinds of learning but, understandably, they often fail. The combination is much scarcer than its elements. When they do succeed in finding the scarce combination, schools use it as if it were not scarce at all. The experienced teacher is required to act as skill model and as practice partner for individual students, to say nothing of the many duties which are unrelated to learning or teaching. The scarcest skill of the teacher is usually the ability to diagnose learning difficulties, a skill acquired by observation of learning under various circumstances. In school, the use of this scarce skill must share time with all of the other functions built into the teacher's role. This is how schools succeed in taking plentiful learning resources and making them scarce. They package them all together, then stand the package on its head.

What schools do, nevertheless, provides an excellent model for the organization of educational resources. The model has merely to be used in reverse. Educational resources must be administered independently of each other, and given priority in reverse order to that of the school. First, attention must be given to the availability of information in the form of records, the instruments which produce and interpret these records and other objects in which information is stored. Second priority must be given to the availability of skill models, people who can demonstrate the skill to be acquired. Third priority must go to the availability of real peers, fellow learners with whom learning can actually be shared. Fourth and last priority must go to the provision of educators who by virtue of experience can facilitate the use of the more essential learning resources. It might appear that educators are of first importance, if only to see that the other resources are properly valued and used. It is evident, however, that this is what educators when incorporated into schools do worst, not because they are educators, but because schools give them powers which corrupt their judgement.

Skill models are different from educational objects in two important respects. First, they must personally consent to their use as educational resources. Second, they frequently have enough additional flexibility and other secondary advantages to make it worth the trouble of gaining this consent. In this technical age they are not strictly necessary, since their skills can all be demonstrated on records of one kind or another, but they are convenient. The superior flexibility of human models was recently demonstrated in Patrick Suppe's experiment in computerized instruction at Stanford University.[1] The computers were programmed to teach reading and numbers to beginning first graders. The computers worked well – so long as one teacher stood behind each child to deal with his unexpected responses. Typical of these was the insertion of a pencil under the keys which operated the computer. The computer could, of course, be programmed to deal with each one of these unanticipated reactions but at the end of the third year of the experiment the programmers were lagging further behind the children than at the beginning. Computers may be able to teach other computers but it appears that human learners may, for a time at least, continue to be better served by human models.

Skill models are in plentiful supply. There are almost always more people in any vicinity who possess a particular skill than there are people who want to learn it. The major exceptions are when a new skill is invented or imported into a new territory. When this happens, skill models proliferate rapidly and are soon in balance with the demand for their services. Only schools and similar monopolistic institutions make skill models scarce. Schools try to forbid the use of models who have not joined the teachers' union. Some of the most famous musicians in the world, who fled from Germany at the time of the Nazi terror, were not allowed to teach music in the schools of the United States. Unions and professional associations also restrict the unauthorized use of skills, frequently creating serious shortages of vital services. Nurses, for example, are scarce in the United States, primarily because the training curriculum has been extended again and again by schools of nursing, placing the cost of training beyond the means of the girls for whom the profession offers opportunities for social mobility. Restrictions on the practice of a skill are usually justified in terms of professional standards and protection of the public. Sometimes these claims are true, but more often they are patently false. The best skill models are frequently those who have just learned a skill. Children learn to read from older siblings, sometimes with ridiculous ease. English schools were really economical for a time, when Joseph Lancaster introduced the systematic use of older students to teach younger ones. This system was better than schools usually are and was very much cheaper. It shares with other forms of schooling the fatal flaw of not allowing the learner to choose his model, his subject matter and his place and time of instruction.

Skill models should be organized as an educational resource so as to give each learner the widest choice of models and each model the greatest latitude in accepting or rejecting learners. This requires first an absence of restrictions and second a directory of skill models of all kinds. Ideally, there would be no special restrictions of any kind. Model–pupil relationships are subject to risk and abuse as are any kind of human relationships but the general laws and customs which cover all such relationships provide the best available protection. Learning in and of itself creates no additional hazards. The advantage of permitting the learner to seek and find a model from whom he will learn is, in general, worth all the additional risk that such latitude entails. Not learning what needs to be learned is likely to involve the greatest risks of all.

Developing directories of skill models is not intrinsically difficult. Truly convenient and comprehensive directories might be so valuable, however, as to warrant considerable investment. Responsibility for developing and administering such directories should probably be vested in a public utility. Skill models willing to offer evidence of their skills would be offered free registration. Those who chose not to do this would, nevertheless, retain the freedom to make such arrangements as they could, using their own means of publicity.

The financing of skill training contracts can best be dealt with after the organization of other educational resources has been discussed. It may be that skills which seem to be required for intelligent participation in the modern world should be taught at public expense. In this case the public utility which maintained the directory of skill models could also be charged with paying them. Public payments should not be made, however, except upon evidence that an essential skill had been learned to an acceptable standard. Private contracts could be left to the wishes of the contracting parties.

Having learned a skill, people need someone with whom to practice. But peers are important even before practice. Who would bother to learn a skill unless there were others with whom to share it, fellow explorers of the new ground opened by the skill? Many skills are learned primarily with peers, taking advantage of the skill models in the general environment. Often peers and skill models are hard to distinguish. In ordinary interpersonal relations there is no need, nor advantage, in distinguishing skill models from peers. On the contrary, learning occurs best when such distinctions are not made. There is, however, an important distinction which can be ignored only if the individuals involved are willing to ignore it. Peers are, by definition, equals deriving mutual benefits from their relationship. They can play tennis together, go exploring together, study mathematics together, or build a camp together. If they are peers, they contribute more or less equally to each other's objectives. Helping a smaller brother or sister learn what he wants to learn is different. It may be equally enjoyable for a while, but the enjoyment palls more quickly. Peer relationships are freely chosen, freely kept. Skill modelling frequently requires some sort of compensation for the model, if the relationship is maintained as long as the learner would like. A method for compensating skill models is needed, therefore, which is not needed in relationships of peers.

Finding peers is merely a matter of knowing where they are and being able to get there, write or call on the telephone. Neighbourhoods free of automobile hazards are all that most children need for the purpose. As skills develop, however, the better ball players go farther afield to find worthy competitors, the botany bug outgrows his neighbourhood pals, the serious ballet addicts find their ranks thinning out.

Schools supplement neighbourhoods, as things are now organized, but schools create as many barriers to peer groups as opportunities for them. In schools, peer groups form around the goals of teachers or around the interests of dope-pushers. Student-initiated groups have a hard time competing with either. But for teenagers the neighbourhood no longer serves as an adequate base for contacts. If it did, the telephone and the automobile would be more dispensable. These instruments are often charged with breaking up the face-to-face community, but actually, along with *Main Street* and *Peyton Place*, they mainly expose its limitations.

For adults, with their frequently highly specialized interests, even the largest cities cannot always provide true peers. The best illustration of this is the scientific community, which must be world-wide for the most fruitful peer encounters to occur. The scientific community also illustrates how peer matches can be fostered or frustrated.

The logical structure of science provides a framework for identifying persons of similar interests. Its journals provide means of communication. Its rules of logic and criteria of evidence provide the parameters for fruitful encounters. Its achievements unfailingly generate new problems which beckon explorers with common interests. All these advantages of science, as a network of related interests which provide an ideal basis for peer-group formation, have now been offset by institutional barriers. National and corporate interests now dictate who may speak or write to whom, in what terms, when, how and where. Only the model of a scientific community is left, available for other interest groups which have been less successful in forming fruitful peer groups than scientists used to be.

The advantages of science in fostering communication among peers are no more natural than the forces which have now disrupted them. The modern 'logical' structure of science did not exist a century ago. Neither did its current journals, nor its present rules of logic or standards of evidence. The beginnings were already there but, two centuries ago, even those were only dim foreshadowings.

Fortunately, other communities of interest do not have to retrace the steps of science. Her example, as well as her products, make it possible to shortcut these steps. Today any area of interest can be so described that a computer can match the persons who share it. Learners in search of peers need only identify themselves and their interests in order to find matches in the neighbourhood, city, nation or world. The computer is not indispensable. In the neighbourhood a bulletin board will do, in the city a newspaper, in the nation a national magazine, in the world an international journal. All of these media and others are and should be used to find peer matches, but computers can make the matching easier and more flexible.

The operation of a peer-matching network would be simple. The user would identify himself by name and address and describe the activity he wanted to share. A computer would send him back the names and addresses of all who had inserted similar descriptions. People using the system would become known only to their potential peers.

As in the case of skill models, a public utility might provide free service for the finding of peers. This would be justified not only in educational terms but also as buttressing the right of free assembly. The same right should also be extended to include prohibition of involuntary assembly, in the form of compulsory attendance at school. If freedom of the press and free assembly were taken seriously and public means provided to make them available to everyone, compulsory school attendance, military service and other common current compulsions would become unnecessary.

As schools are replaced by networks of educational objects, skill models and peers, the demand for educators, rather than declining, will increase. These educators will perform different functions from those now performed in school and not all of them will be the same people. The need for people with real ability in administration, teaching and scholarship will increase, and their rewards in terms of educational achievement, professional freedom and income will also increase. Schoolmen whose skills are primarily in the hiring, supervision and firing of teachers, public relations with parents, curriculum making, textbook purchasing, maintenance of grounds and facilities and the supervision of inter-scholastic athletic competition may not find a market for their skills. Neither will all of the baby-sitting, lesson-planning and record-keeping teachers, unless they have skills which can be turned to other uses, or unless they leave education for more honestly designated employment.

At least three kinds of professional educators will be in strong demand: first, architects and administrators of the educational resource networks which have been briefly described; second, pedagogues who can design effective individual educational programmes, diagnose educational difficulties and prescribe effective remedies; and third, leaders in every branch of learning.

Educational resource networks are simple in principle and will be effective only if they are kept simple in operation. The kind of simplicity required, however, is frequently the mark of genius. People who can multiply the services available to people and still stay out of their way are relatively rare. 'You always find the other kind', in the words of an old refrain.

The designers of the new networks will have to understand knowledge, people and the societies they live in. They will have to be dedicated to the idea of student-directed, individualized education. They will have to understand the barriers to the flow of relevant information and how to reduce them without generating counter-actions which would annul their efforts. They will above all have to be able to resist the eternal temptation of subtly directing the studies of their clients instead of opening ever new and possibly dangerous doors for their investigation.

Teachers were greatly honoured before there were schools, and will be again when they are freed to practise their profession without the constraints of forced attendance, mandatory curriculum and classroom walls. The core of an independent educational profession will be the pedagogue, a bad word now but one which will come into its own when students, parents and teachers are free to make responsible educational decisions. They will find, then, that they need advice and assistance in selecting learning programmes, choosing skill models, discovering peers, finding leadership in difficult endeavours. Unlike the network administrator, the independently practising pedagogue will not have to suppress his opinions and values in favour of those of his client. He will be free to make value judgements because his clients will also be free. He will have no way of shaping their decisions except through the persuasiveness of his advice. And he had better be right as well as persuasive, for his clients will hold him responsible. This profession will not be for the faint-hearted, but the competent pedagogue will find in it the rewards of the old family doctor, the man who made the reputation which modern medical specialists are still living on. There will, of course, be room for many pedagogic specialties, such as testing and educational psychiatry – which will be in less demand as the damage done by schools declines. Eventually the new pedagogic profession may succumb to the over-specialization which now afflicts medicine, but by that time it will have made its contribution.

The role of the educational leader is somewhat more elusive than that of the network administrator or the pedagogue. This is because leadership itself is hard to define. Walter Bagehot's description of a leader, as a man out in front when people decide to go in a certain direction, has not been improved upon.[2] It takes nothing away from the leader who positions himself for relevant reasons.

Leadership, like education, is not confined to intellectual pursuits. It occurs wherever people do things together and especially when the going gets rough. This is when true leadership distinguishes itself, usually depending more on relevant prior learning than on the personal qualities so dear to the world of fiction. There is no valid test of leadership, even past experience. As Thomas Kuhn points out in *The Structure of Scientific Revolutions*, even in fields as rigorous as physical science, the most distinguished leaders are, periodically, bound to be proven basically wrong.[3] There is, on the other hand, no substitute for leadership and leaders remain one of the vital educational resources which learners must be helped to find. Leaders will, of course, recommend themselves and this must be depended upon even in systematic attempts to match learners with leaders.

In practice, there will always be a fuzzy line between skill models and leaders. Both are specific to the content of what is being learned or done; both are subject-matter specialists. Mountaineers cannot substitute for physicists or vice versa. The directories and administrative means that serve to locate skill models can also be used to locate leaders, who will identify themselves by the claims they make, the terms they insist upon, and the behaviour they exhibit in actual encounter. Networks can be helpful in finding potential leadership but the true commodity will always be recognized only after the fact.

There are other kinds of human beings who can be called educational resources only by stretching the concept. These people are, nevertheless, more important educationally than all of the resources described above. They are mothers, fathers, children, lovers and all of the other kinds of people who distinguish human beings from featherless bipeds. These people cannot be treated as educational resources because they are primarily something else. Familial, erotic, economic and political relationships cannot be organized as if their main purpose were educational. All of them, however, have enormously important educational implications which cannot be neglected even though they cannot be manipulated for specific educational purposes. Unless people can enjoy, in the main, good human relationships, they cannot be educated nor educate themselves. The most fundamental educational resource, then, is a world in which most people can have good relationships with others. Perhaps paradoxically, universal education may itself be the principal means of realizing such a world.

It should be emphasized again that distinguishing the various kinds of human educational resources makes sense only in economic and administrative terms. It would be an error for individuals to treat each other or to regard themselves as restricted to one or another of these categories. For economic reasons, however, the distinctions are vital. Whether educational resources are scarce or plentiful, expensive or cheap, depends entirely upon maintaining these distinctions. And this in turn determines whether education, and all other privilege, is to remain the prerogative of the few, or whether education and justice are to be made available for all.

The way to establish an institution is to finance it.
Justice William O. Douglas

12 Financing Education

Any attempt to say who now pays for education and who benefits from it is bound to be incomplete. This is partly because
education is not well defined, while attempts to define it usually
generate more controversy than agreement. The errors of in-
completeness are now reduced, however, by the overwhelming
preponderance of the school. School is the world's largest
enterprise; larger than agriculture, industry or warfare.

Of school's three rivals for the educational dollar, all but one
are demonstrably small by comparison. The mass media are
the most prominent, the easiest to define and probably the
smallest. Large as the press and television are, along with movies,
radio and all other forms of publishing, broadcasting and public
entertainment, they represent less than half the money, time
and clientele involved in schooling.[1] On-the-job training, while
harder to estimate, may be a little closer but still a losing rival to
schools. There are a few more people at work throughout the
world than in school, but not many more. Not enough more to
offset the much smaller proportion of their work time devoted to
learning.[2] Perhaps the greatest rival of schooling is the personal
time people spend in learning outside of institutional frameworks. This time and its imputed value may still exceed even
current investment in schools, but it is very difficult to measure.
One of the worst things that can be said about schools is that they
have made such serious inroads upon this time and that they
threaten to capture it all. This personal learning time is man's
principal hold on freedom, doubly in danger now, first, because
schools threaten to absorb it and second, because schools use up
the resources which could enrich it. A futher capture of the
resources which still go into personal learning could have only
reactionary consequences. It would also be undesirable to try
to capture the resources which still go into training on the job.

Work has been dehumanized too much already by separating it from learning. Better use of educational resources by the mass media is a desirable goal, but it may be that a better educated public is the best way to achieve this. Attempts to achieve it by government control run the risk of further manipulation of the people on the one hand, and of an ineffective cultural snobbery on the other. Only the resources now reserved for the school are open for reallocation among educational objectives, at no loss to any interests except those which seek to perpetuate the present structure of privilege.

There are still people who believe that we could finance the education we need by means of schooling, if only we were willing to give it priority, but this is to ignore the competitive character of schools. No sooner is universal high-school attendance approached than the competition shifts to colleges, at higher costs. There is already agitation for degrees above the Ph.D. on the grounds that the doctorate has become common and degraded. There can be no end to schooling in a world which puts no limits on consumption and where degrees determine people's position at the trough.

Schools are an almost perfectly regressive form of taxation, paid for by the poor to benefit the rich. Schools are supported, largely, by general taxes which ultimately fall more upon the poor than their direct incidence suggests. Property taxes, for example, are paid by those who occupy dwellings rather than by those who own them, excise taxes by consumers rather than producers. Meanwhile, the benefits of even public expenditures for schooling are distributed in direct proportion to present economic privilege.

The children of the poorest one-tenth of the United States population attend school for an average of less than five years. The schools they attend, at this grade level, spend no more than $500 per pupil per year. These children cost the public, in schooling, less than $2,500 each over a lifetime. The children of the richest one-tenth of the population finish college and a year of graduate school, which costs about $35,000. Assuming that one-third of this is private expenditure, the richest one-tenth still get ten times as much of public funds for education as the poorest one-tenth.[3]

Compared to most of the rest of the world, the schools of the United States are relatively fair. In Bolivia, for example, one-half of all public allocations for schools are spent on one per cent of the population. The ratio of educational expenditures on the upper and lower one-tenth of the population, respectively, are about three hundred to one.[4] Most parts of the world are nearer to the Bolivian than to the United States ratio.

Schools constitute a regressive tax because the privileged go to school longer and because costs increase with the level of schooling. Graduate schools, for example, provide by far the highest student subsidies not only in relative but also in absolute terms. Graduate students come largely from the upper income levels of the society. Nevertheless, students pay almost nothing at this level, in fact are frequently paid, while graduate-school support, even in private universities, comes largely from public funds. Costs in the sciences, for example, run up to several hundred thousand dollars per student per year. At the under-graduate level there is a higher proportion of private expenditure but, even here, public subsidies average several thousands of dollars per student per year, as compared with hundreds of dollars at the elementary level, where most of the poor children are.[5]

Schools make it impossible to equalize educational opportunity, even in terms of the allocation of public resources. Unless they abandon scholastic standards altogether, they can never keep poor children in school as long as rich ones and, unless they reverse the cost ratios which have always characterized schooling, they will always spend more at higher than at lower levels. Even compensating programmes specifically designed to help poor children cannot achieve their purpose within the structure of the school. Of three billion dollars earmarked by the federal government of the United States for supplementary services to poor children, less than a third was actually spent on eligible children; these children showed no measurable improvement, while the non-eligible children, with whom they were mixed and who also benefited from the money, did make a measurable gain.[6]

In a just world, or in a world trying to achieve justice, public expenditures on education should be inversely proportional to the wealth of the student. Private expenditures on education are made almost entirely on behalf of the better-off, so that merely equal expenditures on education would require that public funds for education go in a higher proportion to the poor. Even this would not equalize educational opportunity, since the parents and the homes of the better-off represent an investment in their education which would also have to be offset. Finally, the poor suffer the handicap of the culture of silence, the inheritance of magic and myth designed to ensure their continued docility. It is this, rather than deficient genes, which handicaps the learning of their children; this plus the punishment of failure and disapproval which is their customary lot in schools. These disadvantages, not inherent in them and not of their own making, require an additional expenditure on the education of the poor to offset them. If all of the public funds allotted to education in every nation were spent exclusively upon the poor it would still take many generations to offset the handicaps which generations of exploitation have imposed upon them.

It should now be clear that even the first step in equalizing educational opportunity among social classes requires an allocation of educational resources outside the school system. The only ways of making sure that poor children get even an equal share of public funds for education are either to segregate them completely in schools of their own, or to give the money directly to them. The first of these alternatives has been tried and has conspicuously failed. The second provides the key to the proper allocation of educational resources.

Putting command of educational resources in the hands of learners does not solve all problems, but it is an indispensable step toward a solution. Not only the problem of equalizing opportunity across class lines but all of the other problems discussed above become manageable with the aid of this principle. Schools would stand, adjust or fail according to the satisfaction of their clients. Other educational institutions would develop in accordance with their ability to satisfy client needs. Learners would choose between learning on the job and full-time learning, which skills they wanted to learn, at what age they wanted to use their educational resources, and how. This presupposes a system of lifetime educational accounts, administered in early childhood by parents, in which resource credit could be accumulated, and over which the learner, from a very early age at least, would have a veto power.

In the world as seen by Adam Smith, this would solve all of the problems. In the real world, there is still an imperfect distribution of the supply of the real resources required for education and there is, furthermore, imperfect knowledge of what resources are needed and where they are to be found. This imperfect knowledge is not confined to learners. The would-be suppliers of educational resources also lack knowledge of where their potential clients are and of what they need. There is finally the age-old problem of imperfect character; people who want something for nothing and those who will sell anything to make a profit. If perfect competition and complete knowledge existed they would offset the problem of man's venality. Since they do not, it remains to compound the evil.

A system of personal educational accounts and a system of public educational utilities, such as those suggested in the two previous chapters, would mutually supplement each other. They could be combined in a number of ways. One way would be to make the public utilities self-supporting, as the postal system is supposed to be, charging each user for the approximate cost of the service rendered him. Another way would be to make the services of the resource networks completely free. This would require dividing public funds for education between the support of the proposed utilities and provision for the proposed personal accounts.

Besides these alternatives, various mixtures are possible: providing some services free while charging for others, charging some people and not others, according to age, income or other criteria. The possible combinations are too numerous to permit exhaustive discussion but a few are worth considering. The networks might, for example, provide a directory service free, locating skill models, objects, peers, etc., but doing nothing further to facilitate economic access. This would leave it to the learner to buy or borrow the indicated book, or pay the skill model, out of his personal account. Alternatively, libraries and stores of educational objects in common demand might be maintained for the free use of the public; reading and mathematics teachers might be publicly paid to teach elementary skills.

These alternatives contemplate only the use of public funds derived from tax revenues, divided between educational resource networks and personal educational accounts. Additional financial arrangements are conceivable. An educational bank might be established in which educational services could be deposited and from which educational credit could be received. Skill models, for example, might elect not to be paid in cash but to accumulate credit for themselves and their children. Learners might borrow from the bank either credit to pay a skill model who is accumulating credit, or cash to pay one who wants cash, and the learner might later repay the bank either in cash or in service as a skill model for someone else.

An educational bank could not compete in the market with banks less restricted in their activities. Government support for such a bank, or for any free service by an educational resource network, or even for the establishment of such networks, would constitute an educational subsidy. The use of tax funds for education is, of course, already a subsidy, but so long as these funds went entirely into educational accounts there would be no subsidy for one kind of education in preference to another. Today there is. Graduate schools are highly favoured over elementary levels. Science is favoured over other subjects. Nor are subsidies confined to the public sector. Monopolistic industries are able to pass on the costs of educating both their employees and the public, because they can set their prices to absorb such costs. Government bureaus have even greater latitude of this kind. The military have almost unlimited funds for training and almost unlimited capacity to educate the public, not only by spending money but by manipulating information. The mass media are currently subsidized by the advertisers of products and services, while producing corporations in turn are able to charge the public for the education they impose upon them. Some educational subsidies are paid directly out of the public purse. Others are collected by private corporations under permissive public laws. All are expressions of public policy more or less openly admitted.

Educational policy would be most open to public view if all public funds were channelled into personal educational accounts, and all educational institutions, including the proposed resource networks, had to be self-supporting. At present levels of expenditure, this would provide every man, woman and child in the United States with $250 per year to spend on education. It would also force all elementary and high schools, universities and graduate schools to charge tuition high enough to pay all costs. At first sight, many a scholastic career would appear to be nipped in the bud. Each newborn child, on the other hand, would have a lifetime fund to finance his personal education, valued at $17,000. Each twenty year old could count on $12,000, each forty year old on $7,000, each sixty year old on $2,000. This is the average amount of schooling the American public is buying now, through taxes, for each of its citizens.[7] It is roughly equivalent to a college education. The fact that so few people get it merely underscores the inequality of the present distribution. Actually few of those who now receive more would be seriously deprived if public funds were divided equally. All but a few would be able to finance their education privately. Poor children, on the other hand, would have five times as much educational support as they now receive. On the average, these poor children would get the same amount they now get up to age fifteen. They would then, however, still have four times as much left. Many poor children become able to profit from formal training only at about this age, although this may be only because the present system of schooling is so poorly adapted to their needs.

What about those who, today, spend at a much faster rate? Would the average middle-class child who now uses up his quota of public funds by about age twenty-one be retarded by having to keep within his annual quota? Under at least three circumstances he would not. First, his family might supplement his allowance. Current private investment in education is only one-fourth of public expenditure, one-fifth of the total. Second, he might not attend schools but get his education elsewhere at lower cost. Third, he might borrow against his lifetime allowance. Under favourable circumstances this would appear to be relatively safe. If the student's family were fairly well off but reluctant to invest their own money, they could probably, in one way or another, insure against the risk of failure. If, on the other hand, the family were poor but the student able and promising for his chosen career, insurance might be bought at public expense to cover his risk.

What about people who didn't use their allowance? The taxpayers might be allowed to benefit. Allowances might be increased in subsequent years. Families might be permitted to pool their allowances. Adults would probably learn fairly quickly to use what they had coming, and this could work to the great benefit of education, the adults themselves, and their society. Adults acting on their own behalf would be shrewd buyers of education. Their demand would bring educational resources into the market which younger people would also use, once the demonstration had been made. Many now passive middle-aged and older people would come alive and begin to take a more informed interest in their own and in public affairs.

How would educational allowances actually be spent? What would happen to schools? How would profiteering be controlled? Answers depend very much on development of the resource networks previously described. Capital investment in these networks would have to have a prior claim on public funds for education, even though this investment were to be repaid by the fees charged for service. If these networks were well designed and operated they would influence the investments of many learners, especially adults at first. Many of these adults would be parents, however, whose children would also soon begin to use the networks.

Schools would, for a time, continue to be used by parents dependent on the custodial care they offered and by students far enough along to be dependent upon them. Schools could not, however, continue to function at today's level since the public funds available to the age group they serve would be less than one-third of the public funds that schools receive now. A few schools might survive – old established private schools and a few public schools in rich suburbs whose patrons could afford to keep them up and could also afford not to worry too much about the economic future of their children. Most people would soon discover more efficient ways of learning and more pleasant ways of spending time than in school.

Charlatans and profiteers might have a field day for a time. But, if the networks functioned properly, they would soon be checked, not by suppression primarily but by the competition of honest suppliers and skill models, aided by competent pedagogues advising parents and students. Controls of the type offered by better business bureaus would be sufficient, since they would be too inefficient to do much harm but available for use against a real mountebank.

The money which is now so insufficient for schools would be more than enough to support an enormous network of educational objects and to partially support a number of skill models, pedagogues and educational leaders far in excess of the number of teachers employed today. Many would work only part time as skill models and educational leaders, practising their skills and pursuing their explorations for other purposes as well. Pedagogues working full time could serve a clientele of a thousand persons, giving each on the average a couple of hours per year.

Financial magic? Not at all. The cost of custodial care would in large part be transferred back from the public to the private purse. Most of it is now provided for people too old to need it – old enough to work and, in many cases, better off working. The additional education provided, at lower cost, would also produce a citizenry able to solve the pseudo-problem of how to employ the additional 'un-needed' hands and brains released from the tedium of school.

Whereas it appeareth that however certain forms of government are better calculated than others to protect individuals in the free exercise of their natural rights, and are at the same time themselves better guarded against degeneracy, yet experience hath shown, that even under the best forms, those entrusted with power have, in time, and by slow operations, perverted it into tyranny; and it is believed that the most effectual means of preventing this would be, to illuminate, as far as practicable, the minds of the people at large, and more especially to give them knowledge of those facts, which history exhibiteth, that, possessed thereby of the experience of other ages and countries, they may be enabled to know ambition under all its shapes, and prompt to exert their natural powers to defeat its purposes.

Thomas Jefferson:
A Bill for the More General Diffusion of Knowledge

13 The Revolutionary Role of Education

Effective alternatives to schools cannot occur without other widespread changes in society. But there is no point in waiting for other changes to bring about a change in education. Unless educational alternatives are planned and pursued there is no assurance they will occur no matter what else happens. If they do not, the other changes are likely to be superficial and short-lived. Educational change, on the other hand, will bring other fundamental social changes in its wake.

True education is a basic social force. Present social structures could not survive an educated population, even if only a substantial minority were educated. Something more than schooling is obviously in question here; indeed, almost the opposite of schooling is meant. People are schooled to accept a society. They are educated to create or re-create one.

Education has the meaning here which students of education and of human nature have always given it. None has defined it better than Paulo Freire, the Brazilian educator, who describes the process as becoming critically aware of one's reality in a manner which leads to effective action upon it.[1] An educated man understands his world well enough to deal with it effectively. Such men, if they existed in sufficient numbers, would not leave the absurdities of the present world unchanged.

Some such men do exist: men who understand reality well enough to deal with it effectively. Today they exist in small numbers, most of them engaged in running the world for their own convenience, a few in trying to stop them. If, in any society, the proportion of persons so educated were 20 per cent instead of 2, or 30 instead of 3, such a society could no longer be run by a few for their own purposes but would have to be run for the general welfare. The laurels of leadership lose their appeal if spread over more than a few and an educated minority, above a certain size, would have to opt for justice and sanity. Whenever, as in pilgrim New England, ancient Athens or early Rome, a reasonable proportion of the population has been educated, in the sense of knowing what the local score was, their societies have been run not by the few for their own interests, but by the many in the common interest.

Nation states as they exist today could not for long survive an educated population. Nations made up of educated citizens, or containing a substantial minority of such citizens, would tend to merge with other nations. This could, of course, begin to happen within the nominal framework of the nation state. Geographical boundaries would not have to change. If immigration and tariff restrictions change sufficiently, political frontiers become meaningless.

Class distinctions would also tend to disappear in educated societies; as indeed they have tended to do in certain periods of history. This does not mean that individual differences of value-position or privilege would disappear. In a changing society new differences would tend to occur as rapidly as old ones were equalized. It would be difficult, however, to identify differences resulting from fairly constant change either with class, race, or any other socially identifying label. An educated society would become and remain highly pluralistic, with many loosely related, fluid hierarchies based on a large number of fairly independent value criteria. Some people might be rich, some powerful, others popular, still others loved or respected or strong, but not very many could be all of these for very long.

An educated population would make not only their nations but also their specialized institutions responsive to the needs and desires of clients and workers in addition to those of managers. An educated minority of any size would never put up with current health and education services, environmental pollution, political policy control by military-industrial cliques or advertiser control of mass media, to say nothing of traffic jams, housing shortages and the host of other absurdities which afflict modern societies.

No educational magic is implied. Not even educated people could solve these problems in their present context. What they could and would do is recognize an impossible context and change it. They would realize, for example, that competitive consumption is an impossible way of life for more than short periods or small minorities. Once this were grasped, much of our present production and employment would be seen as not only unnecessary but actually harmful. War materials are an obvious case, but schooling, pretentious short-lived consumer durables, advertising, corporate and governmental junketing and a host of other products and activities are scarcely less so.

What makes it so difficult to do anything about these matters is that the present way of life of so many privileged people depends upon keeping things as they are. Education alone cannot solve this problem. It can help people to see what shifting sand their present security rests upon. It can help them visualize feasible alternatives, although something more may be required to realize them. This is merely to say that education alone cannot bring about revolutionary social change.

Theories of political revolution provide some basis for a more general theory of institutional revolution, but important revisions and additions are needed. Political institutions are uniquely based upon power and the use of violence. In political matters, ideology and rationality tend to be subservient to the use of power and violence. In the case of other institutions – even including the religious – ideology and rationality are relatively more important. This may not always be apparent in the declining days of decadent institutions bolstered by naked power. It is nevertheless true that people choose their markets, their schools, their hospitals and transport, somewhat less blindly, somewhat more in consideration of costs and benefits – including sentimental attachments – than they do in choosing and defending their citizenship. Changes in non-political institutions are, at least on the surface, subject to rational discussion. Major changes in non-political institutions are at times carried through without violence, although this might be less the case if legitimate violence were not a monopoly of political institutions. It is conceivable, at any rate, that revolutionary change in non-political institutions could take place without violence, could be semi-rational, could be affected by analysis, research, debate, legislation, resource allocation, market behaviour and peaceful political participation. Socialization in the Scandinavian countries and Britain and the formation of the European Common Market provide examples of changes that have taken place in relative peace, though certainly not without pressure and the threat of violence.

Scientific and religious revolutions are worth looking at for ideas. In mature sciences, one major theory controls research and teaching in the field until gradually its deficiencies become more and more widely recognized, it fails to satisfy an increasing set of requirements made upon it, and is finally discarded in favour of a more successful rival. The necessary conditions for this kind of peaceful change are easy to identify. There is a common language which members of a branch of science use and jointly understand. There is regular communication among scientists. There is an ultimate court of appeal, namely empirical evidence produced under controlled and published conditions. Finally, there are agreed upon canons of reason and logic. These conditions are hard to match outside the mature sciences but they provide useful standards which have actually been approximated in the examples of peaceful institutional change cited above. Thomas Kuhn's recent book and the controversy it has engendered show that even scientific revolutions are vastly oversimplified in the above account.[2] They do proceed without major violence, however, and with an apparent rationality, at least after the fact.

Religious revolutions have not commonly been peaceful but some have been, and these illustrate an important principle. They show that something comparable to loss of faith in an old version of truth, like that which occurs in a scientific community, also occurs among the rank and file of a population. New religious faiths have swept over large areas at a rapid rate, and the conditions under which this has happened have something in common, both with each other and with the conditions under which scientific revolutions have occurred. Sweeping religious movements have always occurred among miserable people, under deteriorating social conditions leading to disillusionment and despair. The other condition for their occurrence has been a powerful and attractive new revelation of truth. Sometimes, but not always, charismatic leaders and disciples have proclaimed the new truth. As in the case of science, common language, communication and commonly accepted standards of reason and logic are necessary conditions for a religious revolution. The logical standards are not, of course, the same as those of science and the ultimate test of truth is very different. Evidence for the emotions, not evidence for the senses, is the touchstone of religious truth. Deeply felt needs must be satisfied. Nevertheless, the parallels between scientific and religious conversion are much more impressive than the differences. Religious revolutions, too, may hold lessons for a theory of institutional revolution.[3]

The annals of violence itself may support the idea that violence need not accompany change. Military history is full of instances of battles which were not fought because one side had a demonstrable preponderance of power. Usually this was the side that began with the most power, but not always. A peaceful revolution is not one in which the holders of power give up meekly. This is truly romantic nonsense. A peaceful revolution is one in which the nominal holders of power discover that they have lost their power before they begin to fight.

There is no assurance that institutional revolution can be peaceful. There is only a hope and not necessarily a very good one. The peaceful character of revolution is not, however, the only consideration. It is important partly because of its critical relation to an even more important criterion. This is that revolution be effective, that it achieve its purposes. The history of political revolution is a history of betrayal, both of the idealists who helped create the conditions for it, but even more of the common people on whose behalf it was made and who themselves made the major sacrifices. Revolution will result in only those positive changes which are in the course of being made when the revolution occurs. If it consists in nothing but these changes, so much the better.

He that will not apply new remedies must expect new evils.
Roger Bacon

14 Strategy for a Peaceful Revolution

Whether a peaceful revolution is possible only time will tell; it may be in some countries and not in others. The necessary conditions for it, however, are easy to state. It cannot occur unless most people are persuaded that it should, nor unless the verdict of this majority is accepted. However, it is unlikely first, that a majority could be persuaded of the need for revolutionary change while control of the mass media and the powers of the state remained committed to the status quo, and second, that a minority holding these powers would yield them peacefully even if convinced of its minority status.

An educated minority of substantial size could, under certain conditions, create a majority in favour of revolutionary change. This could happen only if there were deep disillusionment with existing institutions and a compelling formulation of alternatives. The following attempt to show how these conditions might be brought about in the area of education is obviously no blueprint for revolution. It is merely a sketch of a possible series of preliminary steps.

The first step is already implied. Large numbers of people would have to become disillusioned with schools. This is currently happening, but the numbers are not nearly large enough, nor is the disillusion deep enough. The basic contradictions of the school system must become publicly apparent: that schools are too expensive to serve as a universal system of education, that schools perpetuate inequality, that schools inoculate the vast majority against education by forcing unwanted learning upon them, that a schooled society is blinded to its own errors. The contradictions are there. To get them generally recognized is difficult, since the people most looked up to are the most schooled. It is always difficult to recognize what has been done to you, when the recognition is itself degrading. Unless this recognition occurs, however, nothing else can.

The programme described below assumes that deep and widespread disillusionment with schools *will* occur. If it does, the following proposals for legal, fiscal, institutional and educational programmes will become progressively more feasible and these, if carried out, will themselves help to speed the loss of faith in schools. People hang on to what they recognize as very faulty institutions until they see what else they can do. While they hang on, it is difficult for them not to rationalize their actions by hoping that things are not as bad as they seem.

On the legal front, a two-part strategy is needed: the first consisting of action under existing laws, the second of proposals for new legislation. Some kinds of legal action already have a long history, especially the objections to compulsory schooling traditionally associated with dissident religious sects. More recently, such defence has been based upon non-religious grounds, including the claim that children are not receiving the education which schools purport to give. Suits claiming an equal share of public resources earmarked for education have also been filed, based on the promise of equal protection of the laws contained in the fourteenth amendment. Further legal action possible under existing law may be suggested by the following legislative programme.

We need legislation which would parallel the first amendment to the Constitution of the United States, prohibiting any law with respect to an 'establishment of religion'. Institutional monopoly of education, especially by the state, has all of the evils of a state church, compounded by the fact that a secular school system can be made to seem neutral with respect to basic values. Since such a claim is obvious nonsense, the defence of a national school system falls back upon the overriding needs and prerogatives of the state. But this involves a contradiction with democratic theory, which holds the state to be the instrument and not the moulder of its citizens. The school, in modern times, has become more powerful than the church of the middle ages. The career and, therefore, the life of the individual depends upon his success in school. The law makes him a criminal if he does not attend it. He is subject to its influence far more than medieval man was ever subject to the church. The case for a prohibition of educational monopoly is stronger than the case against a state church, which in times of crisis could oppose the state and claim heavenly authority for its position. The claim for academic freedom is the nearest schools can come to a similar role and we have recently seen how relatively feeble it is. Churches, on the wane, did infinitely better against the Nazis and Fascists than universities, in the fullness of their power. The school is completely an instrument of the state and creates subservience to it.

Along with prohibition of an established school we need to extend our anti-discrimination laws to include schooling. We must forbid favouritism based on schooling as well as on race or religion, and for the same reasons. Where and how one has been schooled is as irrelevant to one's capacity to do a job as race or religion. All affect aspects of job performance which are of interest to the employer but which the law has decided, in the cases of race and religion, are not his legitimate concern. Neither is the school the job applicant went to, nor whether he went to school at all, if he can demonstrate the ability to do the job. We are so used to schools that this statement appears strange, yet the logic is simple. We now reserve the best-paid jobs for those whose training has cost the most. If schooling were privately financed this might make limited ethical sense, but its economics would still be ridiculous. The public has, indeed, been schooled to believe that a more expensive item must be better, but economists explain this on the assumption of price competition among suppliers. Schools have precisely the opposite kind of competition. Even Harvard would be suspect if it were cheap.

We would have to distribute educational resources in an inverse ratio to present privilege in order to equalize educational opportunity. The argument against such a policy is that it would spend the most money on those with the least aptitude and would produce the least total education. This argument can be challenged, since aptitude judgements are based on success in a school system which discriminates against the poor. But in the end such arguments will not decide a political issue. Most people believe that public resources are equally shared and if not that they ought to be. A law requiring equal sharing of public educational resources is, thus, a third item in a legislative programme. A system of individual educational accounts would be the only feasible way to enforce such a law.

These three laws would effectively disestablish the school system as an educational monopoly. They would not prevent the development of a new one. By creating an educational market they would open the way to already powerful economic institutions which might easily take advantage of their power to establish a new educational monopoly.

Effective extension of anti-monopoly laws to the field of education would, therefore, be a necessary fourth legal step. Since such laws are now relatively ineffective in many other fields, this step would be far from routine. The weakness of anti-monopoly legislation is no accident; its enforcement would threaten the present system. This illustrates the more general principle that revolutions are not made by passing laws. Litigation and legislation can play only a part in a revolutionary strategy, and even that only if properly supported by economic, institutional and educational programmes.

If the best way to establish an institution is to finance it, then one part of a strategy to replace schools is obvious. The obvious is not, however, always easy. We are, for one thing, talking about a great deal of money. The combined public-school budgets of the world total almost as much as is spent on armaments and soldiers. If student time were given its market value it would come to much more. This much money will not be liberated from its present channels unless very attractive alternatives can be found. Fortunately, not only educationally but politically attractive alternatives exist.

Public funds for education might be redirected to students, teachers, taxpayers or businessmen.

Educational accounts would channel funds which now go directly to schools through the hands of students. Students might still spend them on schools, either because the law gave them no option or because the schools succeeded in hoodwinking them or because the schools, under the impact of necessity, succeeded in delivering the goods. In all probability, schools would get a steadily declining share of the educational dollar if it went directly to students.

Students would probably elect to spend some of their dollars directly on teachers, bypassing the schools, but there are also other ways in which teachers could profit at the expense of schools. Any significant weakening in the regulatory power of school would tend to have this effect; their power to compel attendance, for example, or to certify compliance with curriculum requirements. If students were to receive credit by examination without attending classes, teachers would be in increased demand as tutors. For them to increase their earnings would, of course, require a transfer of the savings resulting from reduced school attendance to a tutorial account. Most school laws would not have to be changed to make this possible.

One way of transferring funds from schools to taxpayers is merely to reduce the resources earmarked for education. Another way, however, is to shift educational emphasis from children to adults. Since there are more taxpayers than parents, education distributed over the adult population would tend to match educational benefits with tax liability. The taxpayer, of course, would get back a dollar earmarked for education in place of one which had no strings attached, but this might have good educational by-products. The taxpayer would insist upon maximum control of his dollar and would spend it on education valued by him rather than dictated by another.

There are several ways to shift the educational dollar from schools to businessmen. Educational accounts are one. Performance contracts are another. Such contracts have recently been written by a number of schools with entrepreneurs who guarantee to teach a testable skill and who are not paid unless they do. Still another way to benefit business is to shift the burden of teaching from people to reproducible objects, be these books or computers.

There is an understandable reluctance on the part of educational liberals to make common cause with taxpayers and businessmen. Some academicians claim, for example, that mass media, especially television, already have more educational influence than schools and that weakening the schools would merely strengthen the hold of business interests on the minds of men, women and children. Galbraith even argues that the academic community is one of our main hopes of escaping the worst implications of the new industrial state. The evidence does not support him. There is no major issue – war, pollution, exploitation, racism – on which the academic community, as such, has a discernible stand. There are intelligent courageous men in schools and universities, as there are elsewhere, but they receive no effective support from their institutions. In the exceptional case when an institution has shielded an unpopular dissident, it has also muffled his voice. The worst causes, on the other hand, have had no difficulty in recruiting academics to their support while institutions of learning have entered into contracts with all kinds of other institutions for all kinds of purposes.

But this does not meet the argument that jumping out of the school fat might land us in the television fire. If one believes in people and in freedom, this would still be a step forward. No one is compelled to watch television and everyone knows who is talking and why. People learn if they are given a chance, although not always what we want them to learn. God had to gamble on people and has frequently lost. Without this gamble, however, there would be no humanity.

If educational liberals are unwilling to cooperate with taxpayers and businessmen, they must submit to an ever-waxing educational bureaucracy whose efficiency is steadily declining. If, on the other hand, real education were to result from this proposed unholy alliance, this would in itself reduce the danger of economic domination. Responsibility is best divided between private and public interests if policy is made by those who do not been written by a number of schools with entrepreneurs who do. Taxpayers, businessmen and educational liberals can be satisfactory allies if none are permitted to write the rules under which all will operate.

It would be a mistake, however, to conclude that a competitive market in educational resources would necessarily result in good education. If everyone were already educated it might, but this is to assume the end we are seeking. Starting from where we are, certain educational institutions would have to be subsidized.

One of the most important tasks would be to induce parents and employers to reassume their proper educational responsibilities. Every thinking person knows that real education occurs primarily at home and at work, but a number of facts have conspired to rob this truth of its former general acceptance. The modern organization of society in offering free schooling rewards both parents and employers, in the short run, for reducing their normal educational roles. Schools benefit politically potent parents, while business gains from any reduction in production costs. Similarly, the competitive consumption in which modern households engage induces them to save on costs for which there is nothing to display. Except perhaps in certain kinds of academic households, bright children are harder to show off than shiny automobiles.

This kind of dominantly economic competition among producers and households is itself the product of a particular kind of legal structure. Until this is changed, some kind of special inducement, some kind of subsidy, will be needed to put educational processes back where they occur most rationally and economically, in the home and on the job.

Another place where a great deal of effective education used to occur was in the practice of the arts. Before modern technology took over, all production involved the practice of art. What we now call the fine arts were integrated with the practice of other crafts, and people learned not only by working with more experienced masters but also from associates practising related arts. In the early stages of industrialization, now rapidly passing, this kind of learning was disrupted. It could now be re-established, since the demand for industrial labour is rapidly declining, but only if people who learn, teach and practise the various arts are given a dependable claim on the goods and services produced by modern technology. Unrestricted competition between men and machines is not a natural phenomenon, but one which has been deliberately engineered in modern societies. Most countries of the world are frustrated in their efforts to bring this competition about. Modern countries may find it no less difficult to undo, but they must undo it if the arts are to reclaim an educational role which can in no other way be performed. There is no comparable way of teaching everyone the essential skills of hand and foot, ear and eye, mind and tongue.

In addition to the revival of traditional educational institutions, the modern world requires new ones, both to make available to learners the objects they require and also to make available the human assistance they need. Some of these institutions have been described as networks, or directories of educational objects, skill models, learning peers or professional educators. A public utility designed to match educational resources with educational needs could be self-supporting, once established. It might even be established with minimum public investment, but some experimental operation and testing would probably be required for it to reach its full potential.

Schools cannot be disestablished and education made freely available to all while the rest of the world remains unchanged. Competition among nations, classes and individuals will have to be replaced by cooperation. This means placing limits upon what any individual or group can consume, produce or do to others; limits which are being widely transgressed today by many individuals and groups. Acceptance of such limits implies an increased self-insight into what the real interests and possibilities of groups and individuals are. More than that, it implies a sacrifice of short-term interests for those which are more enduring. This is not the kind of behaviour for which the human race is noted. It remains quite probable, therefore, that it will not be learned except under the impact of catastrophe – if then. There is no need, however, to plan for catastrophe. There is every need to plan for its avoidance.

The final and critical component of a strategy for peaceful educational revolution is education iself. People have been schooled to regard an unschooled world as fantasy. Alternatives which lack the familiar characteristics of schools have an unreal aspect to a schooled mind. From what kind of fulcrum, with what kind of lever, can the required change in perspective be achieved? One answer is the school system itself, and efforts to change it. Today's disillusioned students, teachers, taxpayers and administrators include those who have tried and failed to change the system. The architects of educational revolution will be recruited from these ranks.

Paulo Freire provides the educational means by which the revolutionary rank and file can be assembled. Poor people, black and white, peasant and urban proletariat, can learn to see what schools so obviously do to their children. Taxpayers can learn to interpret the meaning of trends in the costs of schooling. Even the privileged, oppressed by the stink of pollution and their growing fear of the poor, may come to wonder why they did not learn about these things in school. If they do not, their children are likely to tell them. These children of the privileged may turn out to be the teachers of the educational revolution. Not all of them, for many seek inconsistent goals. Oppressed by the hypocrisy around them, they seek the truth. But they also seek the warm social womb which a technological world denies them. Some will find one, some the other, perhaps most neither. Since the total number of dissatisfied students can only increase, enough may eventually find the truth.

Today's educational tasks do not, in the main, require genius but they may require heroes. Some room for talent, if not genius, remains. To bring the truths of modern science, economics, politics and psychology to the masses without simplistic distortion will take some doing. Nevertheless, the sincere desire to do this remains a scarcer commodity than the ability. There are good reasons why desire, great enough to lead to action, should not be in plentiful supply. Those who seriously undertake to bring truth to those who because of their large numbers are most capable of bringing fundamental change – such people run a considerable risk. The Gandhis and Martin Luther Kings do not die in bed. Che Guevara took weapons into the jungle with the intent to arm followers who could protect themselves and him. He was, beyond doubt, a hero and a martyr. Those who go armed only with the truth will be still more dangerous and also more vulnerable. No one, while he himself remains safe, can in conscience call for heroes. But the heroes have always appeared and – when the time is ripe – will again.

One makes the revolution because it is the best way to live.
Danny the Red

15 What Each of Us Can Do

Most of us are not cut out to be heroes, but heroes will be of no avail unless we support them. What we can all do, and must do if there is ever to be a just world, is to begin to live as we would have to live in such a world. If this sounds as if it has been said before – it has. Every great religious leader has said it in one form or another. This makes it neither untrue nor irrelevant but is, on the other hand, the best evidence of both its relevance and truth. If it promises no new magic, guarantees no ultimate victory, but claims only to put humanity back on the main path out of the past, this also is evidence of its truth and relevance.

Power and security, whether based on magic, religion or science, have always been false beacons leading to the repeated shattering of human hopes. They are false because the attainment of either ultimate power or security would be the final end of everything worthwhile in human life. People have repeatedly pursued these goals – the prophets of Israel called it idolatry – but people have also, again and again, recognized their idols and turned away from them.

Our modern idols are science and technology and their temples are the institutions which propagate their worship and profit from the proceeds. The promise of this modern cult – every man a king, with his private palace and his royal chariot – has captured the fancy of most of mankind. Suppose, even, that it were realized. What would there be to do? Only an endless exchange of royal visits, comparing the quantity and quality of royal johns, and an endless drag race of royal chariots, starting from countless crossroads. Eliminate the crossroads, with over and under-passes, and the whole point of the game would be lost. It would be like checkers with the red and the black playing on separate boards.

But this dream of universal royalty is a pipe-dream – only a few can win. Does that make the game worth playing? Not for those who lose. And for those who win? Already they are establishing private arsenals in their suburban redoubts and servicing their Cadillacs with bottled air while they drive through valleys of smog which grow longer and wider and deeper by the day.

So what can people do? They can begin to live as they would have to live in a sane, just world. They can begin again to guard their health, avoiding poisonous air, water and food and the over-eating and under-exercise which more than defeat the miracles of modern medicine. There are other millions, of course, who under-eat and over-exercise because they are forced to work so hard in order to eat at all. What can they do? They can do different things depending on whether they have the cooperation of the affluent or not. In either case it comes to a matter of sharing – but sharing can be mutual or unilateral.

People can either increase or decrease their consumption and production, depending on whether they are now doing more or less than their share of the world's work and using more or less than their share of the world's goods. They can share their possessions or their needs. They can conserve, among other things, the natural environment they live in.

Lowering consumption, sharing and conserving are three actions most of us can take and yet, jointly, they constitute a powerful revolutionary programme. Consider the consequences if this programme were consistently practised in Europe and North America only by those who believe in its principles.

There would be an immediate sharp drop in demand, especially for the more elaborate goods and services. Ever since the Second World War, production in the North Atlantic community has been directed more and more to the sale of luxury goods, including food, clothing, shelter and transport for those already fed, clothed, sheltered and transported much better than most. No small part of the problem of the American economy today is the failure of young people from the upper middle class to establish themselves in the style their parents would gladly support. If only those who share the basic values and beliefs of these young people would follow their example, the market for automobiles, housing and appliances would collapse. The resulting unemployment would involuntarily curtail the consumption of other people, who would then come to see on what a false foundation their pseudo-prosperity had been built. For these people, sharing and conservation would at first be forced consequences of involuntary unemployment but once – or once more – experienced they would begin to recommend themselves on their own merits.

Sharing and conservation, applied especially to goods which are supposedly durable, would vastly multiply the economic effect of a mere curtailment of excess consumption. Conserved and shared, there is enough clothing, shelter and transport in the North Atlantic community to last for a decade. Much of it would need repair and improvement, but this could be supplied without generating much demand even for new raw materials.

Exchange of services, rather than their purchase, whether voluntary or forced, would further deflate the market for goods, services, raw materials and land. The gross national product of the United States could be cut in half without any reduction of goods and services which actually benefit anyone. What would happen to the foreign commitments of the United States under these circumstances is another matter, but most of the people of the world would be better off if these commitments were curtailed. What now looks like a scarcity of real resources in much of the world would turn out to be an ample supply, with only the problem of rational use and distribution remaining to be solved. Once faced directly, stripped of its deliberately obscuring façade, this problem too might be rationally attacked.

This last statement makes more sense if we remember the political psychology of the great depression. During the 1930s, masses of people became aware of the contradictions involved in some people owning and controlling what they could not use and other people needed. Only the Fascist movements saved Europe from the consequences of this insight and only the war saved America. Would Fascism occur again if conspicuous consumption broke down for a second time? The fear and even the covert threat of this prospect keeps many otherwise constructive people immobilized. But only those who do not learn from history are fated to repeat it. Learning does not mean that because one opportunity is missed all others must be foregone.

This is not intended to minimize the dangers which a breakdown of the present system, absurd as it has become, would necessarily entail. These dangers are great and any way of minimizing them should certainly be grasped. They cannot be avoided, however, by pretending that they result merely from calling attention to the need for basic change or by pretending that the only change needed is to improve the operation of our current institutions. These institutions are basically unsound. They are designed not to meet people's needs but to keep people under control. It would have been safer to change them in the 1930s before we had the atom bomb. It is safer to change them now than to wait until still more esoteric weapons are invented. The risks of change are great but the risks of delay are greater.

What, it may be asked, is to prevent the defenders of the status quo from again using totalitarian nationalist parties, international provocation and war as the means of preserving or re-establishing the present order? Certainly nothing will prevent them from trying. Only enough people deeply committed to a world of sanity and justice, cooperating wisely in their efforts to achieve such a world, would have any chance against those who will assuredly use all means to perpetuate their power and their privilege. But the power of élites declines rapidly when they are forced to rely on violence. They lose the support of even those of their fellows who enjoy their privilege but are unwilling to purchase it once they become aware of its true price. There is no doubt that those who fight for justice, even passively, will pay a price in heightened suffering if privilege is challenged. But the history of Europe during the last great war provides many examples of how people can protect each other even in the face of overwhelming power ruthlessly applied.

No one can know in advance how, in his own case, the battle will be joined. In some places, mere withdrawal from excessive consumption and peaceful sharing and conservation in cooperation with likeminded people will produce a majority capable of taking power by legal political means. In other places, civil disobedience as practised by Gandhi and Nehru in India and by Martin Luther King and his followers in the United States may be necessary. In still other places, the guerilla tactics which characterized the resistance in Nazi-dominated Europe from

1940 to 1945 may be forced upon people who refuse to continue to support injustice. Strategy and tactics at the three levels of democratic politics, passive resistance and guerilla warfare have some important things in common. They all depend upon cooperation rather than coercion. They depend upon local as opposed to central leadership. They depend upon a relatively equal sharing of burdens, responsibilities and rewards. But these are also characteristics of a sane just world. This is how a worthwhile, viable world will have to be run. People will, therefore, learn how to run it in the course of bringing it about.

There is probably no other way of creating a society which is of, by and for the people than through personal cooperation in which each person first orders his own life, in the light of shared principles, and then cooperates with others who share these principles. This is how all communities which have enjoyed a reasonable period of sanity and justice have been established – the early United States, Costa Rica and Uruguay, the ancient Greek and Roman republics, to name only those which I know something about.

The Soviet state and the first French Republic, established on even nobler principles, but by the replacement of one central power with another, were never able to enjoy the fruits of the sacrifice entailed by their revolutions. Their struggles for power engendered, predominantly, new struggles for power. No sooner was power and responsibility concentrated than their downfall began, even in the case of communities originally founded on voluntary cooperation.

What individuals must do, then, is not merely to curtail consumption, share and conserve. They must also learn how a just world is organized and governed. For while a great deal is known about past attempts, none of these attempts succeeded and, thus, evidently not enough was known by those who made them. They were all helped to fail by power seekers who did their successful best to corrupt them, but they were also helped to fail by the neglect, over-confidence, laziness, interest in other matters and, perhaps most of all, by the ignorance of their members. Brutus and Cassius understood the danger that Caesar represented, but they were too few. Jefferson understood and tried to share his understanding by universalizing education, but was betrayed, unwittingly perhaps, by Horace Mann and other inheritors of the public schools he pioneered.

Perhaps the most important single thing that individuals can do is to take back their responsibility for the education of their children. Children learn very young how power is used by the strong in their relations with the weak and it is at least possible that this early learning shapes the individual's behaviour in all of his subsequent relations with those who are stronger or weaker than he.

There is so much that each of us can do to create a just world that the problem is not one of elaborating the ways but rather one of defining principles of selection. One thing that all ways have in common is some kind of sacrifice. The affluent must enjoy less than they could enjoy. The poor must demand more than they can safely demand. Everyone must learn ways of living and perceiving which are new to him, must risk his own security to help his neighbour in trouble. Affluent parents will have to deny an automobile for each teenage son and daughter. Poor parents will have to vent their frustrations elsewhere than upon their children. Both will have to allow their children to take risks from which they could protect them.

A strategy of sacrifice must necessarily be selective. People can consistently sacrifice only those things for which the reward exceeds the sacrifice. Especially is this true since the strategy of sacrifice here described is as necessary after the revolution as during the heat of the battle. A just society cannot first be won and then enjoyed. It must be won anew every day and must, therefore, be enjoyed while it is being won.

For sacrifice is not opposed to enjoyment but is its proper *alter ego*. Health, strength, love and respect, for example, can be enjoyed only while being earned – or for the briefest time thereafter. Even wealth and power are easily squandered.

Each individual, then, must choose the kind and degree of sacrifice which he can sustain, which for him is rewarding. Some must even be allowed to sacrifice their earned share in a sane just world. Most people, when they come to understand what is at stake, will not find it so difficult to choose a burden they can bear with pleasure – a discipline they can enjoy. What follows is not intended to restrict but to amplify these choices.

One form of sacrifice which many people find rewarding is to trade quantity for quality. When, as frequently happens, this entails choosing the products of artisanry over manufactured goods, the revolutionary consequences in an industrial society may be very great. There is no doubt that manufactured goods are cheaper, in most instances, so that more can be enjoyed for a given amount of money. But one original painting may give more satisfaction than a dozen prints and this can be true even though the painter is a member of the family. The principle holds for food, clothing, furniture, home construction and the assembly of jalopies from junk-yard parts. Among the affluent, hobbies can generate demand for tools and new materials more expensive than the finished products. They do not have to, however, nor need art be left to hobbies. It can be a way of life for entire communities and could be used to advantage by and for the poor on a scale not yet imagined.

The average American household, the top 80 per cent, contains not less than a thousand dollars' worth of unused durable goods which with a little work could be made more useful and attractive than goods the poor can afford to buy new at the prices they have to pay. This represents a potential capital of four thousand dollars for each poor American household, the transfer of which would benefit the affluent – they could use the space – the poor and the entrepreneurs who effect the transfer. These entrepreneurs would probably have to have a social rather than an economic motivation or else a very good façade. Too crass an approach might foul the wellsprings of 'charity'. Nevertheless, the use of the term entrepreneur is not mere allegory. There would not only have to be middlemen to effect the transfer in question, but thousands of them might come from the ranks of neighbourhood businessmen who cannot compete, in the sale of new goods, with nationally organized chains.

In addition to its stock of unused goods, the average affluent American household has several thousand dollars' worth of unused space, above what is usually needed for its part-time members and occasional guests. If this excess space were fully utilized, the poor could be as well housed as the affluent. Complete utilization may be hard to imagine but there are many ways in which a substantial part of this space could be salvaged which would benefit everyone except real-estate speculators and snobs. Much of this idle space is owned by older people whose families are grown and gone and who cannot sell because the families who could buy do not meet the ethnic requirements of their neighbours. This problem could be overcome by enough acceptable people willing to buy houses as agents for those who suffer discrimination. Another large block of housing space is immobilized because people are afraid to rent rooms or apartments to tenants they feel might expose them to unpleasantness or even danger. This problem could also be overcome by a proper matching of home owners and tenants.

The two tactics suggested in the paragraph above are opposed in the sense that the first is based on deceit while the second is based upon restoring trust. This does not make them incompatible. If both were used successfully in the same neighbourhood, each would result in the more complete use and, therefore, in the greater value of the neighbourhood. Nor are the two tactics politically incompatible. Most people understand the distinction that a man's home is his castle, in which he should be able to choose his associates, while his neighbour's home is not. Nor are the two tactics morally incompatible. It is not that the end justifies the means but rather that the means chosen in each case appear to be the best available. If this is not actually the case the suggestions are invalid.

This principle for the selection of means has a broad range of application. Even the law against murder recognizes the right to kill in self-defence or in the defence of others. There are few judicial systems, anymore, which would convict a Jean Valjean for stealing bread to avoid starvation. New laws, on the other hand, complicate current choices. Should people send their children to schools which actually harm them even though the law requires that they do so? Should not people help those who are suffering political persecution even though the law has labelled them criminal? Neither the law nor the prevailing moral code provides a fully dependable criterion for action. In Nazi Germany, both law and current morality required people to collaborate in the murder of their Jewish neighbours. When such major issues as power and privilege are at stake both laws and mores are used as weapons.

Nevertheless, neither private morality nor the slogan of political revolution – that the ends justify the means – will do. Choosing the best available means is not itself a foolproof formula. But there may often be no other way of choosing courses of action than to apply relevant economic, political, strategic, legal or moral criteria to the available choices. There may be no better guide to choosing and applying the criteria than that others agree they would be chosen and applied in the sane, just world which is the goal of action.

A third principle is implicit in the above idea of the best available means, namely, the principle of cooperation. It is essential for people to choose and to act as individuals since only the true consent of individuals can validate the concept of justice. Nevertheless, purely individual action is ineffective and hard to sustain. Individuals must find ways of acting together, but they must personally choose these ways rather than be coerced by superior power. Leadership there can and probably must be, but the leaders rather than the followers should be drafted and should follow the policies of those they lead.

Cooperation which results in community, physical or functional, has especially great advantages. The future world must be based on community and, throughout most of the modern world, community has been lost. Even the traditional communities which remain may have to be done over since it is doubtful that people, given a real choice, will settle for the drudgery and hierarchy which characterizes most traditional communities. But there are also important strategic advantages in community effort. Communities can often legitimately take over much of the law-making and police power. They can also serve as examples of sanity and justice to the outside world.

In all of the above there is, obviously, nothing new. Even what may seem original is merely a new dress on an old-fashioned idea. We have become used to thinking of reality in terms of pentagons and atom bombs or, before that, in terms of armies, navies, banks and corporations. People's movements are thought to belong to the dark ages. Yet the oldest part of the United States is less than two hundred years old; the independent nations of South America have scarcely more than a century of history, while those of Africa and Asia, including Israel, were founded by popular movements only a few decades ago. The Vietcong, among others, seem to have a pretty good thing going right now.

It is true that, up to now, military action has often been decisive, but the present rulers of China won their battle with weapons captured from the enemy, while in India there was no military showdown at all.

Three things are new which lend substance to what used to be, and still is called, Utopian dreaming. First, drudgery is out of date. Second, modern institutions require increasingly universal cooperation. Third, universal education is now possible. It was only yesterday that the labour of four people was required to feed five. England had to fence people off the land in order to fill her factories. Today most people are in the way, both in the factory and in the field. Food and all other physical products can be produced more efficiently without them. People are indispensable, however, as passive clients and supporters of the production complex; taking what they are offered and doing what they are told. Without their cooperation, the current system for control of production and distribution would collapse. Increasingly people are becoming aware of these facts: realizing that their bodies are no longer required for mass production and that they are being asked instead to surrender their judgement and their will to its dictates.

But to whose dictates? Production is a mindless thing. It knows no imperatives as to what shall be produced, where and when and for whom. The invisible hand is somebody's hand behind the curtain. More and more people are beginning to realize that they should be deciding these things, along with others, and that actually everyone has an equal right to decide them. When everyone understands this, universal education will be well on its way. There will still be a lot to learn. How to do one's share, how to claim one's share and no more, how to cooperate with others in things which cannot be done alone. These lessons will never be completely learned but when everyone has a reasonable opportunity to learn and to apply them, things will begin to move.

All this, if it were mere exhortation, would still be whistling in the dark. But things are happening. Charles Reich, in *The*

Greening of America, says that a people's revolution has begun. Young people all over the world are tuning out the system and turning themselves on. Older people, including many who are concerned by the tactics of the young, still share their sense of the absurdity of the world they live in. The deprived, especially those who live in the prosperous countries, are opening their eyes and flexing their muscles. The great masses of the deprived, in Africa, Asia and South America, are still largely quiescent. When they begin to stir the thunder may at first roll softly but it will be heard. We can turn it on.

Notes and References

Introduction

1. In 1961 Ivan Illich, Feodora Stancioff and Brother Gerry Morris founded C I D O C, originally called the Center of Intercultural Formation, in Cuernavaca. During its first six years the centre was mainly devoted to educational programmes for missionaries to Latin America. This period ended at about the time Illich published an article called 'The seamy side of charity' in the Jesuit magazine *America*, which called into serious question the very idea of sending North American missionaries to the Third World countries. Since 1967 C I D O C (Centro Intercultural de Documentacion) has concentrated on the analysis of various modern institutions, especially schooling. During this period, C I D O C has hosted the seminar on alternatives in education which I direct.

C I D O C is a meeting ground for people who want to teach. It has no curriculum, grants, no certificates or credits, imposes no academic requirements upon learners or teachers. Students and teachers come to C I D O C from all over the world, with the majority from North America. Dialogue occurs in English, Spanish, French, German, Portuguese and occasionally in other languages. Oral Spanish is taught intensively as a skill.

2. The current rate of population increase in Costa Rica is three times the current world rate (United Nations, *Demographic Statistics, Annual Reports*).

3. George Dennison, *The Lives of Children: The Story of the First Street School*, Random House, 1969.

4. Jonathan Kozol, *Death at an Early Age*, Penguin, 1968.

5. Floyd H. Allport, *Institutional Behavior*, Chapel Hill Press, 1933.

Chapter 1

1. Enrolment figures by grade, compiled by UNESCO, show that only in a minority of even those more advanced countries which have such data do more than a small fraction of the students enrolled in the first grade complete elementary school (UNESCO, *Enrolment Data, Annual Reports*).

2. For a further development of the 'ladder' image of society see the concluding chapter in Raymond Williams, *Culture and Society, 1780–1950*, Chatto & Windus, 1958; Penguin, 1961.

3. *The Public School*, an illustrated report, Department of Public Instruction, Commonwealth of Puerto Rico, 1967.

4. *The Public School*, 1967.

5. Monographs, International Institute for Educational Planning, Paris.

6. From data compiled by the Organization for Economic and Cultural Development for member countries (Paris). See, for example, *Background Study No. 1*, for the Conference on Policies for Educational Growth.

7. This estimate is based on two studies commissioned by the United States Office of Education in 1969. Two groups of educators, working independently, were asked to set forth the currently unmet needs in American elementary and high-school education. The costs of meeting these needs were then calculated in terms of current unit costs as published in the USOE annual report. These statistics have not been published but their results were made available by Kenneth Parsley, Director of the Office of Organization and Methods of the USOE, Department of Health, Education and Welfare, Washington, DC.

8. Frederick Harbison and Charles A. Meyer, *Manpower and Education: Country Studies in Economic Development*, McGraw-Hill, 1965.

9. Analysis of demographic data in many developing countries shows that the number of children born to women during their total child-bearing period declines markedly for women with more than four to six years of schooling, especially in urban areas. A detailed study of declining birth rates in Japan shows that while schooling and urban residence are both related statistically to lower birth rates, the most critical factor is a shift in the vocational basis of family

support from traditional rural to modern urban occupations (Irene Taeuber, *Population of Japan*, Princeton University Press, 1958).

10. From data compiled by the Economic Commission for Latin America, Santiago de Chile.

11. Richard Hoggart brilliantly describes the psychological effects of schooling on scholarship students recruited from England's working class in *The Uses of Literacy: Changing Patterns in English Mass Culture*, Chatto & Windus, 1957; Penguin, 1958.

12. John Holt, *How Children Fail*, Pitman, 1964; Penguin, 1969.

Chapter 2

1. It is only mothers who have been freed from the drudgery of food production and preparation who find it necessary to turn the care of their children over to others. This is because of other differences between modern and traditional societies. Older children are taken out of the home by the school, fathers go to work, grandparents and other members of the extended family are left behind in rural or older urban settlements. Were it not for the school, child care in the modern family would fall exclusively upon the mother. Schools thus help to liberate the modern woman, but only by imprisoning her child and by tying her and her man more tightly to their jobs so that they can support the schools. Women clearly need not only the liberation schools provide but much more. Men and children, however, need liberation too. The same point holds for blacks and others who suffer special discrimination. While each group must formulate its own demands and fight its own battles, unless they also join forces with other oppressed groups they can win only battles, never the war.

2. *Digest of Educational Statistics 1968*, U S Government Printing Office, OE-10024-68.

3. In this light see the history of labour opposition to high schools in Merle E. Curti, *The Social Ideas of American Educators*, Littlefield, Adams, 1959.

4. R. Gurjoy, unpublished paper read at the Conference on Development Planning, sponsored by the Public Administration Department of the State University of New York, held at Saratoga Springs, 11–24 November 1969. For similar evidence see the various books of R. D. Laing.

5. Paul Bady, 'L'enseignement en Chine', *Esprit*, January 1971, pp. 73–88.

6. Michael Young, *The Rise of the Meritocracy*, Thames & Hudson, 1958; Penguin, 1961.

7. John Kenneth Galbraith, *The New Industrial State*, Hamish Hamilton, 1967; Penguin, 1969.

8. Arthur R. Jensen, 'How much can we boost I Q and scholastic achievement?', *Harvard Educational Review*, Winter, 1969.

9. A. S. Neill's Summerhill and schools patterned after it may be partial exceptions. They still, however, teach dependence on the school.

10. W. Dennis and P. Najarian, 'Infant development under environmental handicap', *Psychological Monographs*, vol. 71, no. 7.

11. The failures of ghetto schools in the United States are detailed in more documents than can be listed. Among them are: Coleman, *Report on Equality of Opportunity in Education*, U S Department of Health, Education and Welfare, U S Government Printing Office, Washington, D C, 1966; Herbert Kohl, *36 Children*, Gollancz, 1968, Penguin, 1971; Jonathan Kozol, *Death at an Early Age*, Penguin, 1968.

12. The failures of Brazilian rural schools are best illustrated in the dropout figures. More than half drop out before the beginning of the third grade and according to many studies, conducted by U N E S C O among other organizations, dropouts at this level have not achieved functional literacy.

13. Paulo Freire and Paul Goodman, two current philosophers of education, proceeding from quite different premises, both provide carefully reasoned support for this point of view. Paulo Freire is a Brazilian educator known for his success in teaching peasants to read and write effectively with a minimum investment of time and facilities. A gross over-simplification of his position is that people learn only in the process of becoming conscious of their true life situation, eventually seeing this situation clearly under circumstances which permit them to act effectively upon it. Schools could never provide their students with the action potential which this programme requires. It is interesting that Dewey called for something like this action potential in his proposed experimental schools which never actually came into being.

Goodman's position, in equally over-simplified form, is not easily distinguished from Freire's. Goodman holds that people learn what they need to learn in the course of real life encounters. Professions and trades are learned by practising them. Scholars develop in communities of scholars. Schools can teach only alienated knowledge:

knowledge divorced from both its origins and its applications and
therefore dead knowledge.

The effect of transmitting dead knowledge, according to Freire, is to
domesticate rather than educate. Domestication is training in
conformity and the development of either magical or mythical
attitudes toward those aspects of life which contradict the pressures
toward conformity. According to Goodman the attempt to transmit
dead knowledge either has no effect or leads to a sense that the world
is absurd. Both men are probably right. The real world of the
Brazilian peasant is perhaps too grim to be seen as absurd and must,
therefore, be either repressed or enshrouded in magic. The New
Yorker, on the other hand, may be protected enough to be able to
view the grimness of his world through the semi-transparent veil of
absurdity.

Paulo Freire, 'The adult literacy process as cultural action for
freedom', *Harvard Educational Review*, vol. 40, no. 2, 1970,
pp. 205–25. Paul Goodman, *Growing Up Absurd*, Sphere, 1970.
Joel Spring, unpublished lectures on Marx and Dewey,
CIDOC, 1970.

14. The first United States census which included Puerto Rico, in
1910, showed a majority of the adult population of the island, less than
10 per cent of which had ever attended school, to be literate.
Examination of any census series in which literacy and schooling are
reported shows similar, if less extreme, contrasts.

15. Coleman's *Report on Equality of Opportunity in Education*
shows that home background, including the education of
parents, explains much more of the difference in student achievement
than the quality of schools attended by these students, as measured in
costs, teacher preparation, etc.

16. Analysis of achievement-test scores for all students who took high-
school algebra in the Puerto Rican public schools in 1964 shows a
random distribution of answers on all items except the four or five
easiest, which were essentially simple arithmetic problems. Other
student populations may do somewhat better, but both Project Talent,
conducted by N. Flanagan at the University of Pittsburgh, and
Torsten Husén, *Achievement in Mathematics in Twelve Countries*
(International Educational Achievement Association Project of the
Institute of Pedagogy, Hamburg, Germany) show that differences
between school systems and between countries are relatively small.
Item analyses are not available for these other populations.

It will be noted that statements of fact, in the text, are frequently
supported with Puerto Rican data. This is partially because the author

worked for fifteen years with Puerto Rican school data, but also because very few school systems have data as comprehensive, in as much detail, and so well analysed. This, again, is because Puerto Rico has one of the largest integrated school systems of the world. In the United States only New York City's is larger. Another reason is that school systems in general are not given to quantitative evaluation. Puerto Rico has limited resources, but from 1946 to 1968 enjoyed a very progressive government. Finally, its school system had a series of outstanding directors of evaluation culminating in the work of Charles O. Hammil, who is responsible for most of the analyses cited.

17. Jerome S. Bruner, Rose R. Olver, Patricia M. Greenfield, *Studies in Cognitive Growth: A Collaboration at the Center for Cognitive Studies*, Wiley, 1967.

Chapter 3

1. Phillipe Ariès, *Centuries of Childhood*, Cape, 1962.

2. H. I. Marrou, *A History of Education in Antiquity*, tr. George Lamb, Mentor Books, 1964.

3. Torsten Husén, *International Study of Achievement in Mathematics*, 2 vols., Wiley, 1967.

4. Ivar Berg, *Education and Jobs: The Great Training Robbery*, Praeger, 1970.

5. Richard Hoggart, *The Uses of Literacy: Changing Patterns in English Mass Culture*, Chatto & Windus, 1957; Penguin, 1958.

Chapter 4

1. Leon Festinger, *A Theory of Cognitive Dissonance*, Harper & Row, 1957.

2. Joseph M. Hunt, *Intelligence and Experience*, Ronald Press, 1961.

3. 'Another alternative to working-class solidarity offered is the idea of individual opportunity – of the ladder. It has been one of the forms of service to provide such a ladder, in industry, in education and elsewhere. . . . Yet the ladder is a perfect symbol of the bourgeois idea of society, because while undoubtedly it offers the opportunity to climb, it is a device which can only be used individually: you go up the ladder alone. . . . My own view is that the ladder version of society is objectionable in two related aspects: first, that it weakens the principle of common betterment, which ought to be an absolute value; second, that it sweetens the poison of hierarchy, in particular by

offering the hierarchy of merit as a thing different in kind from the hierarchy of money or of birth.' Raymond Williams, *Culture and Society, 1780–1950*, Chatto & Windus, 1958; Penguin, 1961.

4. New knowledge has meaning only in the perspective of the past. Schools were once such champions of this principle that the word scholastic still carries opprobrium in certain circles. Modern schools have done a complete turnabout. They pay lip service to meaning and reserve their obeisance for relevance. Nor can they blame students for this. Having made themselves the gateway to all other secular delights, they cannot wonder that students storm the gates.

Chapter 5

1. Joseph Campbell, *The Masks of Gods*, 3 vols., Viking Press, 1969.

2. H. I. Marrou, *A History of Education in Antiquity*, tr. George Lamb, Mentor Books, 1964.

3. Edward Chiera, *They Wrote on Clay*, University of Chicago Press, 1938.

4. Richard L. Nettleship, *The Theory of Education in the Republic of Plato*, Teachers College Press, University of Columbia, 1968. See also Marrou, *A History of Education in Antiquity*, ch. 6, 'The masters of the classical tradition'.

5. Aristophanes, 'The Clouds', in William Barton (ed.), *The Plays of Aristophanes*, tr. Benjamin B. Rogers, Encyclopaedia Britannica Press, Great Books of the Western World, no. 5, 1952. See also Marrou, *A History of Education in Antiquity*, ch. 4, 'The old Athenian education'.

6. Marrou. *A History of Education in Antiquity*, 1964.

7. David Knowles, *The Monastic Order in England*, Cambridge University Press, 1941.

8. M. H. Vicaire, *Histoire de Saint Dominique*, 2 vols, Cerf, 1957, and W. A. Hinnebusch, *History of the Dominican Order*, Alba, 1966.

9. Kajetan Esser, *Anfänge und Ursprungliche Zielsetzungen des Ordens der Minderbrüder*, E. J. Brill, 1966.

10. H Outram Evennett, *The Spirit of the Counter-Reformation*, Cambridge University Press, 1969; and James Broderick, *The Origin of the Jesuits*, Doubleday, 1960.

11. Paul Goodman, *The Community of Scholars*, Random House, 1962.

12. In addition to the invention of printing, the fifteenth century brought on an expansion of commercial activities which created a demand for a different kind of instruction. 'Reading and writing' schools appeared in England and northern Germany. These were opposed by the clergy, and a compromise was reached under which they were allowed to continue, but forbidden to teach Latin, thus preserving the clerical monopoly on élite education. Luther deplored students going to these schools when, with the breakdown of monastic education and the old church system, studies no longer led to places in the ecclesiastical bureaucracy. In sixteenth-century England the reading and writing schools were establishments in which 'letter writing and practical accounting were taught, for a new class' (Raymond Williams, *The Long Revolution*, Chatto & Windus, 1965; Penguin, 1961).

13. Johann G. Fichte, *Addresses to the German Nation*, Harper & Row, 1968.

14. Cf. Louis René de Caradeux de la Chalotais, *Essay on National Education*, Arnold, 1934, and F. de la Fontainerie, *French Liberalism and Education in the Eighteenth Century: The Writings of La Chalotais, Turgot, Diderot and Condorcet on National Education*, McGraw-Hill, 1932.

15. Cf. Mona Ozouf, *L'École, l'Église et la République, 1871–1914*, Armand Colin, 1963.

16. Merle E. Curti, *The Social Ideas of American Educators*, Littlefield, Adams, 1959.

17. Joel H. Spring, 'Education as a form of social control', the first of a series of conferences given at CIDOC in February 1970, CIDOC document no. 70/221, 1970.

18. Horace Mann, *The Republic and the School: Horace Mann on the Education of Free Men*, ed. Lawrence A. Cremin, Teachers College Press, Columbia University, 1957.

19. Thomas Jefferson, *Crusade against Ignorance: Thomas Jefferson on Education*, ed. Gordon C. Lee, Teachers College Press, Columbia University, 1961.

20. Cf. Michael Katz, 'From voluntarism to bureaucracy in American education', in *Formative Undercurrents of Compulsory Knowledge*, CIDOC, 1970, pp. 2–14.

21. John Dewey, in Reginald D. Archambault, (ed.) *John Dewey on Education: Selected Writings*, Random House, 1964.

Chapter 6

1. Mark Arnold-Forster, 'Poison in the air', *Guardian*, 5 August 1970.

2. Mohandas K. Gandhi, *Autobiography*, Beacon Press, 1957, and *The Essential Gandhi*, ed. Louis Fisher, Random House, 1962.

3. Janet Reiner, Everett Reimer and Thomas Reiner, 'Client analysis and the planning of public programs', *Journal of the American Institute of Planners*, November 1963, and Bernard J. Frieden and Robert Morris (eds.), *Urban Planning and Social Policy*, Basic Books, 1968.

4. Thorstein Veblen, *The Theory of the Leisure Class*, Allen & Unwin, 1925. First published 1899.

5. S. de Madariaga in *The Rise of the Spanish American Empire* (Hollis & Carter, 1947) claims that one factor in Spain's economic decline was the number of people *exported* to Latin America. If true, this merely supports the old saw that there can be too much of even a good thing. But there are major reasons to doubt Madariaga's explanation. First, of the European countries which were large exporters of manpower in the seventeenth and eighteenth centuries, only Spain and Portugal declined, and these only relative to the northern European countries. Not only these two countries but their colonies have not prospered so much as those which received the greatest number of northern European immigrants. The probable explanation lies in the different social structure of Spain, Portugal and their colonies, on the one hand, and the northern European nations and the colonies which they populated – not the ones they ruled – on the other. Spain, Portugal and their colonies remained relatively feudal much longer than northern Europe, North America, Australia, New Zealand and South Africa. The majority of Spanish and Portuguese emigrants did not have the opportunities to acquire land and political power on the relatively more equal basis of the northern European masses. Thus, the Spanish and Portuguese masses have always remained more alienated from their own élites, both at home and in their colonies, than in the case of the northern Europeans. This is true even in Argentina, Chile and Brazil, which attracted many northern Europeans but which remained much more feudal, especially in the distribution of economic and political opportunity, than other areas to which large numbers of northern European migrants went. Many of the early northern European migrants to Argentina, Chile and Brazil succeeded in breaking into the élite but not in changing it, if indeed they tried. Many of them, certainly, have done as much as any Spanish or Portuguese emigrant to restrict the opportunities of even those of their own countrymen who came after them.

6. Gunnar Myrdal, *Rich Lands and Poor*, Harper & Row, 1958; P. R. Ehrlich, *Population Bomb*, Ballantine, 1968; and Alfred Sauvy, *Fertility and Survival: Population Problems from Malthus to Mao Tse-tung*, Collier, 1962.

7. *U N Annual Statistics on Rates of Development and Investment from Foreign Sources.*

8. James C. Abegglen, *Japanese Factory*, Free Press, 1965.

9. Celso Furtado, *Development and Underdevelopment*, tr. Ricardo de Aquilar and Eric C. Drysdale, University of California Press, 1963; Celso Furtado, *Ecomonic Growth of Brazil*, tr. Ricardo de Aquilar and Eric C. Drysdale, University of Califo nia Press, 1963; and Albert O. Hirschman, *Journey towards Progress: Studies of Economic Policy Making in Latin America*, The Twentieth-Century Fund, 1963.

10. Ivan Illich, 'Outwitting the developed countries', *New York Review of Books*, 6 November 1969, and Ivan Illich, *Celebration of Awareness*, Calder & Boyars, 1971, ch. 11.

Chapter 7

1. Alex Bavelas and others have experimented with small groups in which communication is variously channelled. While there is no direct relationship between Bavelas' work and the hypothesis proposed here, there are certain parallels that suggest a possible, common theoretical explanation. Alex Bavelas, 'Task-oriented groups', *Journal of the American Acoustical Society*, vol. 22, 1950, pp. 727–30.

2. As indicated in the quotation that begins the chapter, J. K. Galbraith's theme in *The New Industrial State* (Hamish Hamilton, 1967; Penguin, 1969) parallels in many ways the argument of this chapter. His argument, is however much more detailed and much more carefully qualified. Without the support of Galbraith's documentation the argument presented here would be much less persuasive. Galbraith does not, however, suggest an institutional dichotomy or continuum of the type outlined in this chapter.

In *The Affluent Society* (Penguin, 1962) which is in a sense a companion volume to *The New Industrial State*, Galbraith suggests the need for a massive shift of resources from private to public enterprise. Again, the major difference from the argument of the present chapter lies in Galbraith's much greater caution coupled with an immensely greater documentation of his assertions and better support, therefore, for his recommendations. For Galbraith, all hope seems to lie in a shift in basic values. In the absence of such a shift, little else is possible. He may be right. But this chapter suggests that, if such a shift should begin to occur, there is a programme of institutional development which men could follow, which could lead to something better than battle between institutions and humanistic social goals.

3. G. William Skinner, 'Marketing and social structure in rural China', in (ed.), *Peasant Society: A Reader*, Little, Brown, 1967.

4. Thorstein Veblen, *The Theory of the Leisure Class*, Allen & Unwin, 1925.

5. It might be argued that electricity, for example, is as addictive as are the household appliances which use it. Judged in terms of withdrawal symptoms this might appear to be so, but a sharper criterion of addiction is the need for ever more of a product in order to produce the same degree of satisfaction. Here electricity, in the absence of appliances or other devices, does not qualify, while the appliances clearly do. Water works the same way. People do not drink more or wash more except as more clothes, better detergents or water-wasting washing machines are introduced.

Chapter 8

1. An oral statement made by Paul Goodman in the course of a seminar held by the International Association for Cultural Freedom at Aspen, Colorado, 29 August to 3 September 1970.

2. Paulo Freire, *Cultural Action: A Dialectic Analysis*, CIDOC document no. 1004, 1970; 'The adult literacy process as cultural action for freedom', *Harvard Educational Review*, vol. 40, no. 2, 1970, pp. 205–25; and 'Cultural action and conscientization', *Harvard Educational Review*, vol. 40. no. 3, 1970, pp. 452–78.

3. See for example Jacques Monast, *L'Univers religieux des Aymaras de Bolivie*, CIDOC document no. 10, 1966.

Chapter 9

1. Suzanne Langer, *Philosophy in a New Key*, Oxford University Press, 1957.

2. Claude Lévi-Strauss, *The Savage Mind*, Weidenfeld & Nicolson, 1966.

3. Harold Lasswell and Abraham Kaplan, *Power and Society: A Framework for Political Society*, Yale University Press, 1950.

Lasswell and Kaplan list four welfare values: well-being, wealth, skill and enlightenment, and four deference values: power, respect, rectitude and affection. In a cross listing of these values they indicate how each is converted into the others (p. 86).

4. 'To be a teacher does not mean simply to affirm that such a thing is so, or to deliver a lecture, etc. No, to be a teacher in the right sense is to be a learner.' Soren Kierkegaard, *Point of View for My Work as an Author*, ed. Benjamin Nelson, Peter Smith Publishers, n.d.

Chapter 10

1. José Ortega y Gasset, *Revolt of the Masses*, Allen & Unwin, 1951.

2. Jane Jacobs, *The Economy of Cities*, Random House, 1967.

Chapter 11

1. The author observed this experiment in person in 1966, saw the attendants behind each child and talked to the computer programmers and to the research staff.

2. Walter Bagehot, *Physics and Politics*, in Norman St John-Stevas (ed.), *Collected Works of Walter Bagehot*, vols. 5 and 6, Economist, 1971.

3. Thomas Kuhn, *The Structure of Scientific Revolutions*, University of Chicago Press, 1962.

Chapter 12

1. National accounts data, U S and other countries, published annually by the United Nations.

2. In comparing the cost of education in school and on the job, all school costs are attributed to the education which occurs in school while only training time on the job is charged to the education which occurs at work. Our analysis of the functions of schooling might appear to invalidate such an attribution and for other purposes it would. For this specific purpose, of comparing educational costs in school and at work, it seems justified. The money the public pays for production is paid for the products of work. The money paid for schooling, so far as the public is concerned, goes for education. In neither case does the public get what it pays for, but in comparing costs it must be assumed that it does.

3. These calculations were made by the author, based on school cost data from the annual reports of the U S Office of Education, supplemented by information contained in such special reports as the Coleman study on equal opportunity. There are no official data on enrolment by family income nor on expenditure by

family income, but there are many bases for estimate and for cross checking the validity of estimates. I believe that I have been, in all instances, conservative and invite others to make independent estimates and to check my calculations.

4. These calculations were made by Ivan Illich, based on official enrolment and expenditure data supplied by the Bolivian Government. They were personally reported by Illich to a specially constituted policy board of the Bolivian Government and were accepted as valid. They reflect, primarily, the fact that only a tiny percentage of the population survives the early elementary grades, and that all the cost of secondary and higher education must be attributed to this tiny minority.

5. Based on compilations prepared by the U S Office of Education, which in turn are based on data reported by the various states, and published annually by the U S O E.

6. Based on an Evaluative Report on U S special allocations for the education of the disadvantaged (Title I) entitled, 'Education of the disadvantaged', published by the U S Office of Education, fiscal year 1968. This report found among other things, that less than one dollar of every three allocated to Title I projects, which were supposed to supplement the education of children whose families had incomes below $3,000 per year, was actually spent on these children. The rest was spent on other children, of higher family income, enrolled in the same school system or on support of the system in general.

7. These calculations are based on projected public expenditures for education for 1971 of $50,000 million. They assume an eligible population of 200 million and an average lifetime of sixty-eight years. *Projections of Educational Statistics*, U S Government Printing Office, O E-10030-68.

Chapter 13

1. Paulo Freire, 'The adult literacy process as cultural action for freedom', *Harvard Educational Review*, vol. 40, no. 2, 1970, pp. 205–25.

2. Thomas S. Kuhn, *The Structure of Scientific Revolutions*, University of Chicago Press, 1962.

3. Norman Cohn, *The Pursuit of the Millenium*, Secker & Warburg, 1957; Paladin, 1970.